GLUTEN FREE

# THE Genius GLUTEN-FREE COOKBOOK

LUCINDA BRUCE-GARDYNE

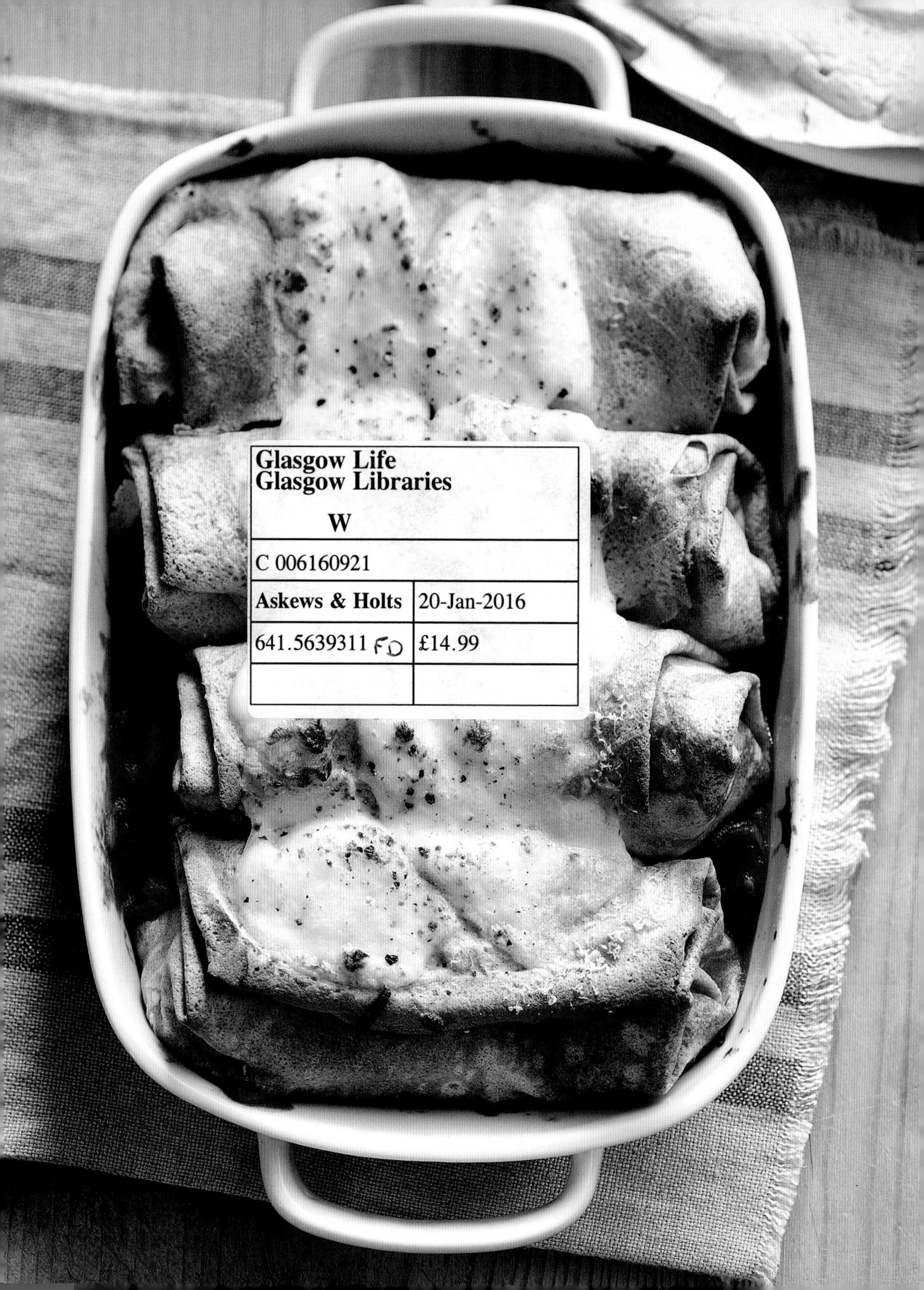

# Contents

# INTRODUCTION

In 2005 my son was diagnosed with an intolerance to gluten, and we were advised to remove gluten from his diet permanently, presenting us with a challenge to continue eating normally as a family. With a scientific background and a passion for food, having trained and taught at Leith's School of Food and Wine and as the author of *How to Cook for Food Allergies*, I decided to take on the challenge of creating a wholesome, soft and tasty gluten-free loaf of bread. After a lot of hard work trying to understand the complexities of baking bread without gluten (breaking two ovens in the process), I finally had a breakthrough and in 2009 founded Genius Gluten Free with the launch of the first fresh and tasty brown and white gluten-free bread on the market.

I have made it my mission to discover, use and enjoy the wealth of gluten-free ingredients available and *The Genius Gluten-Free Cookbook* demonstrates how varied and exciting gluten-free food can be. Whether you have to or choose to live permanently without gluten or simply wish to reduce the amount of gluten in your diet, there is no reason to feel that you are making a sacrifice. This will become clear when you start to make your way through the 120 gluten-free recipes here, covering brunch to party food and inspired by dishes from around the world.

In these pages I explain what gluten is, its role in many of our most commonly eaten foods and why people choose to live without it. I describe how to deal with some of the common challenges associated with gluten-free cooking and the many wonderful and nutritious alternatives that can be used.

I hope this book will inspire you to fill your kitchen cupboards with the wealth of gluten-free flours such as potato flour, wholegrains such as buckwheat and quinoa, pulses including beans and lentils, and ready-made gluten-free staples such as pasta, noodles, breakfast cereals, bakery products and ready-made pastries. The good news is that all these ingredients are available in most supermarkets. Discover the tastes and textures of ingredients you may otherwise never have considered trying. This book dispels the myth that gluten-free cooking is complicated and unpredictable, with a comprehensive section on the many gluten-free ingredients available, their traditional culinary uses and what other dishes they will enhance.

Gluten-free baking and making puddings can cause frustration unless you know how. I have extensively tried and tested the blends of ingredients in the recipes to ensure light, crisp pastry and biscuits and airy, soft cakes. With an understanding of how to blend gluten-free dry ingredients to imitate the behaviour of wheat or other gluten-rich ingredients and tips to help you along, you will be amazed at what you are able to create.

Celebrate the opportunity to live more healthily, cooking from scratch on a more regular basis. This can sometimes be daunting, so cooking techniques are also included throughout the book. Treat your gluten-free diet as an adventure. It is all too easy to stick to the same old wheat-based staples for breakfast, lunch and dinner – and snacks in between.

My greatest wish is that you enjoy making the recipes in this book over and over again because you know they work and because everybody you serve them to really enjoys them. Cooking without gluten does not have to be hard; in fact I have made the job easier for you by writing this book. Join me in spurring people on to look beyond their bag of self-raising flour, wheat bread, and pasta and join in the gluten-free revolution!

# UNDERSTANDING GLUTEN

**Wheat, barley, rye and oats are the most common wholegrain crops grown in the Western world because they grow readily in cold and temperate climates and are extremely nutritious.**

## WHAT IS GLUTEN?

Gluten is a protein that is found in the cereals wheat, barley, rye and oats. The gluten contained in the grains makes them extremely versatile. When the flour of these grains is mixed with water or other liquids, the gluten becomes elastic and forms a stretchy, gluey and kneadable dough that binds mixtures together and creates the open, bubbly structure of bread, the delicate layers in croissants and puff pastry, the light and airy fine crumb in cakes and crisp, shortcrust pastry and biscuits.

Wheat is a key element of the Western diet. This means that gluten is present in many of our common foods, including bread, pasta, pizza, cakes, biscuits, pastry items (pies, tarts) and breakfast cereals.

It can also be found in food we may not expect, such as burgers and sausages, because breadcrumbs or rusk (crushed wheat-flour and water biscuit) are widely used to bulk out the meat. Flour is often added to ready meals, soups and sauces to thicken them.

Barley is prevalent in many of our foodstuffs, such as malt vinegar, food colouring and beer, while rye is added to many cereals.

## WHAT DOES GLUTEN-FREE MEAN?

There are many foods that are naturally free from the protein gluten. These include, meat, fish, fruit, vegetables, most dairy products, rice, potatoes, some grains (including quinoa, millet, corn and polenta) and pulses (lentils, peas, beans). The designation 'gluten-free' is given to foods that contain less than 20 parts per million (20ppm) gluten protein, which is considered a safe level even for people who have a very high sensitivity to gluten. Any product containing wheat or a wheat derivative (e.g. flour, durum, rusk, spelt) will contain gluten. The exception to this is a gluten-free wheat starch called 'Codex wheat starch', which is processed to reduce the level of gluten to below the 20 ppm standard. It is used as a substitute product for wheat flour, to improve the quality and texture of baked gluten-free products such as bread. Although Codex wheat starch contains safe levels of gluten, many people with coeliac disease or gluten sensitivity (see below) avoid buying any product with wheat listed on the label, and many gluten-free manufacturers choose not to use it due to the mixed messages this ingredient generates.

It is important to note that 'wheat-free' is not the same thing as 'gluten-free'. This is because the food product may be made with other elements that contain gluten (e.g. barley, rye) or may have been harvested or prepared with the same equipment used for processing gluten-rich foods, causing cross contamination.

## WHY ARE SOME PEOPLE AFFECTED BY GLUTEN?

There are several ways people can be affected when they eat foods containing gluten.

**Coeliac disease** is an autoimmune condition. When someone with coeliac disease eats a food containing gluten, their immune system mistakes substances found inside the protein as a threat to the body and attacks them. This assault on healthy tissue damages the surface of the small intestine, disrupting the body's ability to absorb nutrients from food.

About one in 100 people are affected by the disease, but only about a quarter of these have been diagnosed. It is hereditary so, if a close relative has coeliac disease, your chances of also having it increases to one in ten. Symptoms can have varying degrees of severity and include bloating, diarrhoea, nausea, excessive wind, constipation, lethargy, mouth ulcers, hair loss and weight loss.

Coeliac disease is a serious, lifelong condition that cannot be treated other than by following a strict gluten-free diet. It is important that you see your doctor for a diagnosis, which involves a blood test and a gut biopsy. Without dietary adjustments, the bowel can become seriously inflamed and unable to absorb nutrition, potentially resulting in associated conditions such as anaemia and osteoporosis. It could also have serious consequences for your health if you assume from your symptoms that you do have coeliac disease, and make the corresponding dietary changes, when these symptoms are actually being caused by something else.

**Wheat allergy** is a reaction to the proteins contained in wheat and is also triggered by the body's immune system. It usually happens very shortly after eating wheat and will eventually subside with the assistance of antihistamines and an asthma inhaler and there is no damage to the gut. Symptoms include rhinitis (a blocked or itchy nose), asthma, skin rash, swelling of the eyes, face and tongue, vomiting, stomach cramps, diarrhoea and, in the most severe cases, anaphylaxis (the term used to describe the symptoms of a severe allergic reaction).

Initial symptoms of anaphylaxis are often the same as the milder allergic symptoms, but can quickly lead to increased breathing difficulties and a dramatic drop in blood pressure, causing dizziness and even unconsciousness. Anaphylaxis is a medical emergency. Without rapid treatment it can be life-threatening. People with a severe allergy to wheat that develops into anaphylaxis carry an auto-injection kit of adrenaline at all times. Complete avoidance of wheat and all products made with it is essential.

**Gluten intolerance** is the term commonly given to reactions that arise after eating gluten-rich foods, but that are not the result of coeliac disease (because there is no immune response or damage to the gut) or wheat allergy. Some people develop symptoms over a number of hours that are similar to those of other digestive disorders, such as inflammatory bowel disease, gastrointestinal obstructions or irritable bowel syndrome (IBS). These can include bloating, nausea and stomach cramps. The medical profession terms this 'non-coeliac gluten sensitivity'. It is not completely clear why the body may have difficulty in dealing with gluten, and there are no specific tests for gluten intolerance. It is often a case of removing gluten from the diet to see whether symptoms may improve, followed by a purposeful reintroduction of a single gluten-rich food at a time to monitor whether symptoms return. Sometimes, given a break from the offending foods, the body can begin to tolerate small amounts of gluten once more.

## The benefits of a gluten-free or lower gluten diet

While it is of course important for those who have coeliac disease or gluten intolerance to avoid gluten, what are the benefits for those who do not? Recent studies have shown that some people find switching to a gluten-free or gluten-light diet can help to ease uncomfortable symptoms of bloating, flatulence and stomach cramps, as well as combating feelings of fatigue – leading to increased concentration, clearer thinking and more energy.

Additionally, for many people, opting for a gluten-free diet has been shown to lead to a higher intake of fibre and a lower intake of salt. When following a gluten-free diet, many people cut out processed foods and move back to 'scratch cooking' – using natural ingredients to cook fresh food for themselves, which is possibly a reason for this. As a result, studies have shown that a gluten-free diet can lead to lower blood cholesterol and glucose levels.

# GLUTEN-FREE LIVING

**With an increasing and more readily available choice of safe foods to eat and greater awareness among others of the issues involved, adopting a gluten-free lifestyle to enhance health and add variety to your diet is now easier than ever before.**

## AVOIDING GLUTEN IN THE KITCHEN

Following a gluten-free diet not only means altering the food that you eat, but also requires some adjustments in how you keep and prepare food. Cross-contamination is the big issue here, so you will need to store safe and unsafe foods apart (a special shelf in a cupboard is adequate) and prepare them separately (gluten-free first) using different utensils and separate cloths to wipe up afterwards. Make sure that everything is clean and that work surfaces have been wiped to remove all traces of unsafe foods. Normal washing-up liquids or dishwashing is effective in removing all traces of gluten after the meal.

## UNDERSTANDING FOOD LABELS

European Union and UK laws (FIR Regulation 1169/2011) specify that fourteen major allergens, including cereals containing gluten, must be clearly listed in bold within the ingredient declaration on the packaging if they are used in the manufacture of packaged food. The list must also make clear when a product uses ingredients or processing aids (such as wheat flour used to roll out dough from rye flour) derived from these major allergens. This makes it easy to spot when a product contains gluten, which is particularly useful when it comes to children. So, for example, a ready meal containing pasta or flour in the sauce must list wheat (in bold) as an ingredient.

Some ingredients containing the fourteen major allergens (e.g. fully refined soya oil, wheat glucose syrups) will not cause an allergic reaction because they are highly processed and the allergen/protein has been removed. These products are assessed by the European Food Safety Authority (EFSA) as not possessing an allergenic risk to the consumer and therefore are exempt from labelling.

Legislation differs in Australia and the USA. The allergens are not declared in bold within the ingredient declaration, but appear in the following format: Allergy Advice Contains: Wheat.

## EATING OUT

Restaurants are now more aware of dietary issues, so eating out need not be a source of anxiety. Whenever possible do a little research beforehand.

### *Tips for gluten-free living*

- Use separate butter/margarine, jam and so on, so that they do not become contaminated by breadcrumbs; you will need a separate toaster or toaster bag too.
- Remember to fry gluten-free foods in a different pan from the others.
- Make sure that you serve gluten-free food with a different spoon from the one you use for other food.
- Keep all unsafe food out of the reach of any children following a gluten-free diet.
- When eating away from home, make sure that the person cooking for you knows what foods contain gluten and follows food-safe procedures; take your own food with you if they seem unsure or unwilling.

## Sport and a gluten-free diet

Whether you exercise professionally or purely for recreation, intake of carbohydrates before, during and after training plays an important role in keeping your energy levels up and regulating your blood sugar, and in helping you to recover afterwards. Carbohydrates are typically sourced from the gluten-rich grains wheat, barley and rye, which are off-limits to those following a gluten-free diet. There is, however, an increasing number of readily available, nutritious gluten-free products to buy on the go and recipes to follow that ensure you can refuel adequately and do not become deficient in the essential vitamins and minerals the body needs for repair.

Some athletes believe that a gluten-free diet actually enhances their performance – and not only because they are free from unpleasant digestive symptoms. Quick (gluten-rich) sources of carbohydrate are often refined or processed (in other words, they can be less nutritious), and have a high glycaemic index (they quickly raise your blood-sugar levels, but not in a sustained way). Those following a gluten-free diet are reliant on foods that are higher in resistant starches and fibre whch possess a lower glycaemic index (they cause a gradual rise in blood-sugar levels over a longer time), giving them energy for greater lengths of time.

If you discover there is nothing you can eat from the existing menu, some restaurants may offer to create something especially for you – after all, it is good for business. Remember that the chef also needs to know how to prepare the food safely, to avoid cross-contamination, and that the sauces and stocks they commonly use often contain wheat flour. Some restaurants list the major allergens on their menus, which saves lengthy discussions at the time of ordering, and most will be understanding if you need to bring individual items such as bread or pizza bases, with you when you dine away from home.

### TRAVEL AND HOLIDAYS

Making sure that you can eat safely while you are travelling can be challenging, as many of the fast-food items that are available will not be suitable for you. By far the safest thing to do is to take your own food with you, particularly 'on-the-go' snacks (see right). This is not always very practical for long journeys and flights, however, but most airlines (with the exception of the budget ones) will be able to provide gluten-free meals if ordered in advance. If you have a severe wheat allergy, you will need to take appropriate medication with you (plus a doctor's letter explaining what this is for). Pack wipes in your hand luggage to clean tables, trays and armrests, and explain your food issues to those around you so that they understand your needs.

Choosing a holiday requires thought, both in the destination and in the type of accommodation. Countries in the northern hemisphere rely heavily on gluten-rich cereals as their staple, for example, and the range of gluten-free foodstuffs that you are able to use at home may not be so readily available elsewhere. In addition, language barriers can make it difficult to get your needs across. Take as many non-perishable snacks and foods with you as you can. Hotel stays may be the most relaxing option for others, but they could be a source of stress and extra effort for you, requiring contact with the hotel in advance to let them know your dietary needs and monitoring of how your food is prepared. Self-catering accommodation can often be the safest bet.

## Easy 'on-the-go' snacks

- Fresh fruit, in particular bananas
- Vegetables cut into bite-sized pieces, such as carrots, and served with hummus
- Nuts and dried fruit
- Gluten-free cereal bars and biscuits
- Popcorn and gluten-free potato and root vegetable crisps
- Gluten-free oatcakes eaten on their own or sandwiched together with pâté or cheese

# YOUR GLUTEN-FREE STORE CUPBOARD

**If you have opted to reduce gluten or omit it completely from your diet, stock up on gluten-free carbohydrates in the form of grains, rice, corn, noodles, pulses and starchy vegetables. These will enable you to create an infinite variety of delicious and wholesome dishes.**

## GRAINS AND CEREALS

Grains and cereals are the most important foodstuffs in the world due to their versatility and high nutritional content. They provide us with a source of carbohydate, protein, fats, vitamins and minerals. Nature has provided many alternatives to wheat, barley and rye, such as rice, quinoa, buckwheat, gluten-free oats, bran and corn. Wholegrain versions are the most nutritious. The fibre, vitamin and oil components are concentrated in the husk of the seed (the bran), the carbohydrate in the main body of the seed (the endosperm) and the protein mainly in the germ of the seed (which generates the new growth). In refined products, only one of these components may be present.

### • RICE

Rice is the most widely consumed cereal for a large part of the world's population, especially in Asia. It can be categorised as follows:

**White rice** is a generic term for long-, medium- and short-rice grains, where the fibrous husk and germ have been removed to create a grain with a delicate texture and flavour when cooked. It provides a neutral base for a wide variety of flavours.

**Brown rice** has long-, medium- and short-rice grains, where the inner nutritious husk, rich in vitamins, minerals and protein, is left intact. The husk gives cooked brown rice a nutty taste and chewy texture, and is perfect for accompanying savoury dishes and using as a base for wholesome rice salads.

**Wild rice** has long, slender grains and a dark brown, chewy outer sheath, which is a rich source of protein, fibre, vitamins and minerals, and a tender, cream-coloured inner grain. Its chewy texture, nutty flavour and colour make it ideal for salads and a good accompaniment for poultry, sausages, salmon, salads and stuffing.

Rice can also be grouped by the length of its grain – long, medium or short.

**Long-grain rice** includes varieties such as Indian basmati rice, Thai jasmine rice and American long-grain rice. All varieties hold their slender shape and retain a clean bite after boiling or steaming. It has a delicate flavour and a fluffy texture that make it a perfect match with robustly flavoured Indian, Thai, Vietnamese and European dishes.

**Medium-grain rice** includes Spanish paella rice, Italian Arborio and Carnaroli rice for risotto, and sticky or glutinous rice, used for Japanese sushi. Medium-grain rice varieties absorb liquid to form rounded, swollen grains. It is ideal with Thai dishes and sweet dishes such as rice pudding and cakes.

**Short-grain rice,** such as pudding rice, is highly absorbent and releases starch into the cooking liquid to form a creamy consistency as in rice pudding.

**Puffed rice** has crisp and light hollow shells made by steaming rice kernels under pressure. It is commonly used in cereals, cereal bars and baking.

**Flaked rice** has white or brown rice grains and is processed through a roller to increase its ability to absorb water and soften. It is perfect for sweet rice puddings and muesli.

**Ground rice** is created from coarsely ground rice grains and has a sandy texture, similar to cornmeal. It is used to make purees for infants, to add a sandy texture to shortbread and as a crisp coating on fried poultry and fish. It is not suitable for baking cakes and pastry, as it creates a gritty texture.

### *Cooking rice*

Although there are a number of different ways to cook rice, my preferred technique is the absorption method because it gives the most reliable results. Described here is the method for long-grain rice (e.g. basmati), but it can be adapted for other types of rice.

Weigh out 50 g rice per person. Pour the rice into a sieve, and rinse under a cold tap until the water running from the rice is clear. This rinses excess starch off the rice grains, which maximises the fluffiness of the rice after cooking. Pour the rinsed rice into a pan large enough to allow it to expand threefold. Level the rice over the bottom of the pan and cover with two parts cold water to one part rice. (For a richer flavour replace the water with vegetable or chicken stock.) Add salt to taste, and bring to a simmer over a medium heat. Cover with a lid and turn the heat down to minimum. After 15 minutes, check the rice – when the water has been absorbed and dimples have formed in the surface, turn off the heat, replace the lid and leave to steam for a further 5 minutes. Drain any excess water and serve.

Brown rice does not require rinsing before cooking. Use the above method, but add three parts water to one part rice, and cook on a very low heat for 40–45 minutes.

Wild rice can be cooked in the same way as brown rice. After 45 minutes the rice should be chewy but tender, and some of the grains will have burst open. Add a little more water and continue cooking for another 10 minutes, or until the rice is cooked.

## • QUINOA

Quinoa is a grain crop related to beetroot, spinach and tumbleweed. It has a mildly bitter vegetable flavour and is a rich source of complete protein, fibre, calcium, phosphorus and iron. It can be served hot or cold as the base of wholesome, substantial salads and as a light-textured bulking agent in stuffing.

### *Cooking quinoa*

Weigh out 60 g quinoa per person, and rinse the grain in a sieve under a cold tap. Put in a large pan, adding three parts cold water to one part grain, and season with salt. Bring to the boil, then turn the heat down to a simmer. Gently cook, uncovered, for 20 minutes, or until the grains have swollen to three times their volume and the water is almost absorbed. Remove from the heat and cover with a lid; leave to steam for a further 20 minutes. When the quinoa has fully absorbed the water, it will be light and fluffy with a tender bite.

## • BUCKWHEAT

Also known as sarasin, this small, triangular seed has a characteristic bitter and nutty flavour, made stronger by roasting. It is most commonly ground to flour or roasted and cracked into smaller pieces (groats) of varying coarseness. Roasted buckwheat groats, called 'kasha', are a staple in Russia and Poland, and are cooked and served like rice. Buckwheat is extremely nutritious, rich in vitamins A and B, calcium and carbohydrate. It is a good substitute for bulgur wheat, which is widely used in Middle Eastern food as the base for tabbouleh and in stuffing and minced meat for kibbeh, sausages and meatballs.

### *Cooking roasted buckwheat groats (kasha)*

Buckwheat is cooked by the absorption method used for rice (see left). Put 50 g buckwheat per person in a pan with twice the volume of water and a pinch of salt, and bring to the boil. Turn the heat down to low and cover the pan with a well-fitting lid. Gently simmer the buckwheat for 12–15 minutes, stirring every 5 minutes, or until the water is fully absorbed and the grain is tender but still slightly chewy.

Basmati rice
Polenta
Chia seeds
Vermicelli noodles
Ribbon rice noodles

Dried chickpeas

Wild rice

Sesame seeds

Haricot beans

Pasta

### • OATS

Oats are members of the grass family and are highly nutritious, providing a rich source of carbohydrates, protein, fat, minerals and vitamin B. When boiled in milk or water, oats swell and release starches and pectins into the liquid, thickening the mixture to a creamy consistency to create porridge. Oats contain a protein called 'avenin', which is similar to gluten. Most people (including those with coeliac disease) can tolerate avenin, but the main problem with oats in a gluten-free diet is cross-contamination, as they are often harvested and processed with the same equipment used for wheat, barley and rye. To avoid this, use only oats where it is stated on the packet that they are gluten-free. With the increasing demand for gluten-free cereals, uncontaminated oats have become widely available and are invaluable for adding texture and flavour to baked foods, cereal bars and cereals, and for coating fish before frying.

**Pinhead oatmeal** is the name given to oat kernel cut into pieces of varying sizes, ranging from the coarsest to medium and fine oatmeal. Pinhead oatmeal, which retains some of the bran (outer husk) takes up to 30 minutes to cook to a soft-textured porridge with a nutty flavour. It is ideal for use in baking and adding a soft, fibrous texture to cereals, biscuits, bread and muffins.

**Rolled oats** are most commonly used to make porridge, as they are highly absorbent and take very little time to cook. They are soft and have a nutty flavour. They are the perfect base for muesli, granola, cereal bars, flapjacks, oat cakes and fruit crumble when baked; they add a wholesome texture to bread, and provide a coating for meat before frying.

### • MILLET

The golden round seeds of millet are a rich source of protein and carbohydrate. Simmer them in salted water until tender, and serve as an accompaniment to stews and curries; use cooled cooked millet grain in salads and stuffing. Millet seed adds texture to baked products too.

**Millet flakes** are fine, golden yellow flakes that add a wholesome taste and appearance to breads. They are used in granola and biscuits, and can be used in gluten-free porridge as an alternative to oats.

### • BRAN

Bran is a rich source of fibre that aids digestion and adds wholesome colour, flavour and texture to baked products and cereals. You can replace bran derived from wheat, barley or rye with a gluten-free bran.

**Rice bran** is the caramel-brown outer husk of rice grains, and adds fibrous texture, colour and nutrients to gluten-free brown bread and cereals. Rice bran is high in healthy unsaturated fats and protein, and a rich source of B vitamins, manganese and iron.

**Oat bran** is the husk of the oat grain and a rich source of fibre, protein, carbohydrate, B vitamins (particularly thiamine and niacin), and minerals such as iron. It has a nutty flavour and fibrous texture, and adds a wholesome taste to bread, pastry, cakes and biscuits. Also add it to muesli for extra fibre.

### • CORN (MAIZE)

The two principal varieties of corn grown for human consumption are sweetcorn, named after the sweet taste of its kernels, and field corn, used to make cornmeal and for corn oil.

**Cornmeal** is produced from grinding dried field corn kernels to a coarse, medium or fine powder. It is known as polenta in Italy. Cornmeal is cooked with water or stock and butter or olive oil to make a smooth purée, which can be eaten warm or be left to cool in slabs, then cut into slices or 'chips' to be grilled or fried. Cornmeal is also used to make cornbread. It is a perfect accompaniment for game, meat or shellfish.

**Popcorn** is made from the kernels of certain corn varieties that explode when strongly heated, forming light and crisp bite-sized pieces. Eaten warm or cold, it can be flavoured with a variety of things. Popcorn is ideal for enhancing the texture and appearance of cakes, biscuits, salads and breakfast cereals when coarsely crushed. Finely crushed, it can be used to coat fish, shellfish or poultry before frying, for a light, crunchy crust.

## NOODLES

Noodles are a staple food in much of Southeast Asia. Traditional wheat noodles are produced from a 'paste' of semolina flour containing ground, gluten-rich durum wheat, water and (often) eggs. Asian noodles can also be made from arrowroot, rice, potato flour or other gluten-free ingredients. They tend to be thread- or ribbon-shaped, in a variety of widths and thicknesses, and add carbohydrate and textures to Asian broths, curries, salads and stir-fries. Fine noodles can be deep-fried until crisp, to be used as a crunchy garnish.

**Arrowroot vermicelli** are very fine white, brittle noodles, usually sold dried in bundles, and can be used in soups and salads.

**Cellophane noodles** or bean thread noodles are made with starch from mung beans. They are wiry, hard and translucent, bought in bundles and soaked in cold water to soften for eating or cooking. Similar, Japanese noodles, known as harusame, are made with potato, sweet potato or rice, as well as with mung bean starch. They can be cooked in sauces or broth or deep-fried for a crispy garnish.

**Rice noodles** look like white ribbon or thread, and are available in a variety of widths; they can be bought both dried and pre-cooked, to be added to soup. Rice noodles work well with sauced dishes or as the basis of stir-fries.

### *Cooking noodles*

Noodles come dried or pre-soaked. Dried noodles need to be softened ahead of cooking by soaking them for 15–30 minutes in cold water, depending on their thickness. Bring a deep pan of salted water to a vigorous boil and lower the drained noodles into it. Boil for the recommended time – this varies depending on the type of noodle. Once the noodles are soft, drain and add to hot dishes at the last stage of cooking, or cool under cold running water to mix with dressings for salads.

Pre-soaked noodles can simply be heated up at the last stage of cooking, either by simmering for 1–2 minutes in a hot sauce or soup, or by stir-frying for 2–3 minutes in the wok with other ingredients.

## PASTA

The quality of gluten-free pasta, made mainly with corn and rice flour, has improved hugely over recent years. It comes in many shapes and is often filled with other ingredients to provide a means of maximising the flavour, texture and appearance of the sauces and other ingredients served with it.

### *Cooking pasta*

The secret to achieving good results is taking care not to overcook gluten-free pasta, as it quickly moves from al dente to a mushy consistency if boiled for too long. Always add gluten-free pasta to a deep pan filled with salted, vigorously boiling water. Closely follow the cooking instructions on the packet, but check the pasta after 7 minutes to estimate how much longer the pasta will require to cook to al dente. Drain and eat soon after cooking because it tends to harden when stored for more than 12 hours.

## PULSES

Pulses offer a rich source of carbohydrate, fibre, vitamins, minerals and protein, particularly when partnered with grains and cereals such as brown rice, gluten-free pasta and bread. They are subtly flavoured, enhance texture and appearance, and absorb the flavours of other ingredients in casseroles, soups, salads and richly flavoured Western and Asian dishes. Available dried, ready-cooked in tins and often fresh or frozen, beans, peas and lentils are part of the pulse family and are a nutritious, filling component of a balanced gluten-free diet.

### • BEANS AND PEAS

Dried beans need soaking in water overnight, before cooking.

**Black-eyed beans or black-eyed peas** are cream-coloured kidney-shaped beans with a characteristic central black spot. Originating is Asia and possibly first cultivated in West Africa, they are grown around the world and particularly in Asia and the warmer regions of North America. They are widely used in Creole and Cajun food, often cooked with rice, pork and hot chilli sauce.

Arborio rice
Pumpkin seeds
Split peas
Potato starch
Flaxseed

Puy lentils

Red kidney beans

Flageolet beans

Roasted buckwheat groats

Quinoa

**Broad beans or fava beans** are native to North Africa and southwestern and south Asia, and grown extensively around the world. These large oval beans are available in both fresh and dried form. Young, tender beans are skinned, blanched and eaten as a vegetable, in salads and pasta. Older beans become floury and hard, and tend to be dried and used in Middle Eastern cuisine, fried in oil and seasoned with spices for snacks, boiled and puréed with spices for dips and sauces, and ground to make falafel.

**Butter beans** were originally grown in the Andes. These creamy-coloured beans are the large variety of the lima bean. They have a soft, floury texture when cooked, make smooth purées for dips and sauces, and work well in mixed bean salads and in rich stews.

**Cannellini beans** are small cream-coloured kidney-shaped beans and are closely related to flageolet and haricot beans. They originate from South America, but are now grown widely across the world. When cooked they have a light, fluffy texture and are great all-purpose beans for salads, soups and casseroles, and rich stews such as cassoulet. They also purée well.

**Chickpeas** are also known as gram or garbanzo beans, and originate from the fertile crescent of Western Asia. They are one of the world's most ancient cultivated crops, widely used across Southern Europe, Africa, India and the Middle East. Dried chickpeas are hard and dense, and look like pale yellow hazelnuts. When cooked they have a firm texture and rich, nutty flavour, and form the basis of many richly flavoured stews and curries in Southern European and Indian cooking. In the Middle East, chickpeas are part of the staple diet and are often cooked and puréed to make hummus or ground into flour to make flatbread.

**Flageolet beans** are used in French cooking. These small, pale green beans are young haricot beans, removed from the pod before they are ripe, then dried. As a result they have a delicate skin, a tender texture and a fresh, delicate flavour. They are best served tossed in butter or olive oil with hearty lamb, veal or chicken stews, or as part of a bean salad.

**Haricot beans** are related to flageolet and cannellini beans. Small cream-coloured beans, they become meltingly tender with slow cooking. They do not have much flavour, but are perfect for absorbing the flavours of the ingredients with which they are cooked. They also add a soft texture to rich and wholesome casseroles and bean salads. Cooked haricot beans make very smooth and delicious purées when mixed with other flavoursome ingredients, to serve as an accompaniment or as a dip.

**Red kidney beans** originate from South America. Be careful when cooking red kidney beans with other ingredients, as they tend to colour them pink. Dried kidney beans need soaking and should be cooked carefully because the outer skin contains toxins, which become harmless with sustained boiling. These colourful beans enhance the appearance and consistency of mixed bean salads and spicy stews such as chilli con carne.

**Soya beans** are native to East Asia, and a number of soya bean varieties are now grown widely across North America and Asia. Unlike most pulses, soya beans are made up of very little carbohydrate and high levels of protein and fat. They are also very rich in minerals and vitamins. Immature fresh soya beans known as edemame are boiled or steamed in the pod and eaten as snacks and in salads. Dried soya beans are very hard and contain toxins in the skin and so require the longest soaking and cooking period of any pulse. They have a bland flavour, but absorb the flavours. Due to their neutral taste, they are used to create nutritious protein-rich staples such as tofu and dairy-free milk, and ground into flour to whiten or soften baked products. Black soya beans are fermented with barley to make soy sauce or processed slightly differently to produce the more delicately flavoured gluten-free equivalent called tamari. Black soya beans are also puréed to make miso, a principal 'umami' flavouring ingredient in Japanese cooking.

**Split peas** are small and cook quickly. They require only 1–2 hours of soaking before cooking. Both green and yellow split peas are used to make the British classic pease pudding, traditionally served with ham. They are also ideal for thickening soups and rich flavoured casseroles.

• LENTILS

Lentils come in many varieties and colours, and are available both dried and tinned. Lentils with their husk left intact retain bite and shape with moderate cooking; lentils without husks tend to disintegrate and are mainly used for thickening soups and sauces. Owing to their small size, lentils do not require soaking and cook in a similar time to rice. This is happy coincidence because cooked together, lentils and rice create a nutritionally complete meal. Lentils are a rich source of protein, fibre, minerals and vitamins, particularly folic acid, vitamin B and iron.

**Puy lentils** from France are tiny, grey-green and have a delicately nutty flavour and a tender, clean bite. They are often served as part of a warm salad or braised dish accompanying fish, sausage and meat.

**Brown and green lentils** are larger and have a more rustic, floury texture; add to rich, meaty stews and thick winter soups.

**Yellow and red lentils** are used widely in Indian cooking, to thicken and add body and nutrition to richly flavoured and spiced sauces. Dhal made with yellow lentils is part of the staple diet in Northern India and Nepal.

## NUTS

Nuts are a very good source of energy and nutrition, containing high levels of protein, carbohydrate, fat, vitamins and minerals. They play an important part in adding flavour and texture to a wide variety of dishes and baked products. Nuts can be subdivided into two categories: tree nuts and groundnuts. The tree nuts most commonly used in cooking include almonds, brazil nuts, cashew nuts, pistachio nuts, hazelnuts, chestnuts, macadamia nuts, walnuts and pecans. The most common groundnut is the peanut (also known as groundnut), which is actually related to the pea family; peanuts are a highly nutritious product, mainly eaten whole as a snack, coarsely ground for sauces for Asian dishes or more finely ground to make peanut butter.

Coarse-ground nuts create a crunchy and flavoursome coating on fried foods, thicken sauces and provide an attractive garnish. Ground to a fine powder, almonds, cashew nuts, pistachio nuts, hazelnuts and chestnuts are an important element of gluten-free cookery. Used as part of a flour blend, they provide moisture, richness, flavour, texture and nutrition to cakes, biscuits and pastry. When the skins are removed, they add tender, subtle texture to baked foods; with the fibrous skin intact, they give fibrous texture to wholesome breads, pastry and biscuits.

## SEEDS

Seeds such as sunflower, pumpkin, poppy, millet, flaxseed (linseed), sesame, pine nuts and chia seeds provide crunchy texture, colour, flavour, protein and fibre, and enhance the appearance of many gluten-free baked foods, cereals and salads. They also make a satisfying snack eaten as they are, blended together or flavoured with other savoury and sweet ingredients. Ground flaxseed adds a fibrous, wholesome quality to gluten-free baked foods and cereals.

## STARCHY VEGETABLES

A number of vegetables with a high starch content can be used to supplement the carbohydrate element of your diet.

**Sweetcorn** is a special corn (maize) variety with sweet, tender kernels. High in sugar and complex carbohydrates, although not strictly a vegetable it is one of the finest sources of dietary fibre and is also full of betacarotene antioxidants, vitamin A, B vitamins and minerals such as zinc, magnesium, copper, iron and manganese. It is best cooked simply: boiled or steamed, and served with a knob of butter, salt and pepper, or wrapped in foil and roasted or grilled on the barbecue. Frozen and tinned sweetcorn stands in for fresh when it is out of season. Baby sweetcorn is subtly sweet and delicately crisp when briefly steamed, boiled or stir-fried, and features regularly in Southeast Asian and Chinese cooking. Store fresh sweetcorn in its green fibrous husk, wrapped in damp kitchen paper, in the fridge.

**Parsnips** are rich in vitamins, fibre and minerals, particularly potassium. A creamy-coloured winter root vegetable, they have an earthy but sweet flavour.

Parsnips add sweetness and soft substance to hearty roasts and stews, and purée to a creamy texture for mash and smooth soups.

**Pumpkins and butternut squash** are the most well known winter squashes, with sweet and juicy yellow or bright orange flesh below the hard skin. They are a particularly good source of fibre, antioxidants, vitamins and minerals. You can use them to make soups, add to stews, curries and risotto, or mash as a side dish. They are also delicious as the principal ingredient in savoury and sweet tarts, pies and cakes.

**Potatoes** are the world's favourite root vegetable and the largest food crop after corn (maize), wheat and rice. Not only are they a rich source of starch, but they also contain high levels of vitamin C, Vitamin B6, fibre and minerals such as potassium, magnesium, phosphorus and iron. Potatoes come in many varieties, shapes and sizes but, most importantly, as 'floury' and 'waxy' types. Keep all potatoes in a cool, dark, well-ventilated place because, if exposed to light, they will turn green and become mildly toxic.

**Sweet potatoes** have a hard cream to bright orange flesh, which becomes soft and smooth when cooked. They have a unique sharp and sweet flavour that goes well with spicy savoury dishes. Aside from being an excellent source of carbohydrate, sweet potatoes are rich in fibre and vitamins A, C and B6. Varieties with a dark orange flesh variety are also rich in antioxidants, including betacarotene. Sweet potatoes are usually peeled, sliced or cut into chunks before baking, roasting or mashing. They can also be added to risotto, pasta or curry.

## FLOUR

Successfully replicating the function of wheat flour in gluten-free cooking involves blending particular ingredients, selected for their range of properties, to create the familiar taste and appearance you expect from a cake, a pastry crust, a slice of fresh bread or a sauce.

**Arrowroot** is a fine white powder derived from the root of the tropical maranta plant. It consists of 80 per cent starch and is used mainly as a thickening agent for sweet and savoury clear sauces. Its fine texture also makes it ideal for use in very light-textured baked products such as short-textured crumbly biscuits and pastry.

**Buckwheat flour** is a greyish-brown speckled flour with a slightly bitter, nutty flavour and is traditionally used to make Breton galettes, Russian blinis and dumplings, American muffins and pancakes, and Japanese soba noodles. Buckwheat is a useful flour for gluten-free pastry, as it helps to bind the dough and gives it a crunch when baked.

**Chestnut flour** is used a great deal in Italian and French cooking in regions where chestnut trees are bountiful. A fine, soft light-brown flour with a gentle, nutty sweetness, it is rich in starch and protein, vitamins and minerals. It adds a natural earthy sweetness and light-brown colour to cakes, bread and biscuits.

**Cornflour or corn starch** is finely powdered white starch extracted from corn (maize) kernels and is widely used to thicken savoury and sweet sauces. Its light texture and neutral flavour make it a highly versatile gluten-free flour in baking, helping to create light-textured cakes, bread, pastry and biscuits.

**Cornmeal** (see also page 14) is made from dried corn kernels that have been ground to either a coarse or a fine yellow sandy-textured flour. It is used widely in North, Central and South American baking to make cornbread, muffins and flatbreads, and adds a sunny yellow colour and short texture to biscuits and pastry. Cornmeal is also used to coat fish and meat before frying to add crispness and colour.

**Polenta** is ground Italian maize, otherwise known as cornmeal, and features as a starchy accompaniment to Italian rich stews and pan-fried dishes. It is cooked by pouring it into boiling stock or salted water, and stirring until smooth while it simmers. Cooked polenta is usually enriched with the addition of butter or extra virgin olive oil and, often, grated Parmesan. It is either served as a soft purée or allowed to set until firm, then sliced and grilled or pan-fried until golden brown and crisp. Set polenta is also cut into batons or 'chips', and baked with olive oil and Parmesan or herbs.

**Potato flour** is a very fine, white soft powder, consisting of pure potato starch obtained from washing out the starch of pulped potatoes. The starch is then separated from the liquid and dried. Potato starch is a neutral-flavoured flour and very important in gluten-free baking for creating a strong, fluffy structure and a light, soft eating experience in bread and cakes such as brownies. It is also an effective thickener of savoury and sweet sauces.

Rice flour is a soft, creamy-coloured flour made from very finely ground white or brown rice grain. Due to its neutral flavour, colour and availability, it is a versatile flour for thickening sauces or coating foods for frying, or as part of the flour blend used to make gluten-free bread, cakes, biscuits and pastry.

Tapioca flour is a fine, white starch powder extracted from the root of the tropical cassava plant. When mixed with water it becomes slightly gluey, lightly binding gluten-free mixtures and making it very effective in lightening the texture of gluten-free bread.

| GLUTEN-RICH PRODUCT | GLUTEN-FREE REPLACEMENT |
|---|---|
| **CONDIMENT SAUCES** | |
| **Soy sauce** made with fermented barley | Tamari |
| **Worcestershire sauce** contains barley malt vinegar and soy sauce | Original Worcester sauce or a gluten-free brand equivalent |
| **Mustard** sauces and some cheaper lines of powdered mustard sauces contain wheat flour as a thickener or add malt vinegar or beer as a flavouring | Gluten-free mustard brands are available, but good-quality plain mustards are usually gluten-free |
| **Brown and barbecue sauce** often contain malt vinegar, and are often thickened with gluten-rich flour | Gluten-free replacements are available |
| **Tomato ketchup**, especially cheaper lines, can contain malt vinegar and flour thickeners | Leading brands are naturally gluten-free, but always read the label before using |
| **Stock cubes** used for thickening and adding flavour to sauces, gravies and soup | Gluten-free stock cubes and gravy granules |
| **Spices and spice seasonings** can contain gluten-rich ingredients, either through cross-contamination in the fields, at the milling stage or in some cases because wheat flour has been added as an anti-caking or filling agent | Buy whole spices when possible to grind yourself, or check the label to ensure that the ground spices do not contain wheat flour |
| **Malt flavouring** is derived from barley malt – a gluten-rich flavouring added to breakfast cereals, biscuits, chocolate confectionery, and drinks and other prepared foods | Black treacle and muscovado sugar are both good replacements for a malty flavour |
| **Ready-prepared cooking sauces** often contain wheat flour. It is often used as a thickener for sauces such as white and cheese sauce, parsley and béchamel sauce and ready-made gravy | Sauces thickened with gluten-free flours are available or follow the recipes in this book |
| **ALCOHOLIC DRINKS** | |
| Beer and whisky are made with barley malt, which is rich in gluten. There is still some concern that spirits made from gluten-rich grain such as wheat or barley can cause sensitivity for people with coeliac disease | Gluten-free beers are now available for drinking and cooking. Replace whisky with spirits made from gluten-free ingredients, such as brandy made from grapes, rum made from sugar molasses and white spirits made with potato, grapes or corn |

Always check the label carefully for gluten before using ready-prepared condiments in your cooking.

# Breakfast & Brunch

A lazy Sunday brunch is a weekend treat. Try making American pancakes with different toppings, or for something more substantial English Breakfast Tulips. For a nutritious start to your day, tuck into my granola, which is packed with gluten-free oats, nuts and seeds.

# AMERICAN PANCAKES

- SERVES 4 – MAKES 8

140 g potato flour
70 g rice flour
70 g ground almonds
2½ tsp gluten-free baking powder
½ tsp salt
2 medium eggs, separated
290 ml milk or dairy-free milk
vegetable oil for cooking

- VARIATIONS:

BUTTERMILK PANCAKES

Replace half the dairy milk with buttermilk, to make pancakes with a slightly sour, complex flavour that cuts through the sweetness of sweet toppings.

LEMON AND SULTANA PANCAKES

Stir the finely grated zest of 1 lemon into the pancake batter.

Pour the batter into a hot greased pan to form pancakes about 7.5 cm across, and sprinkle 6–8 sultanas evenly over each pancake. Once each pancake has puffed and set, turn over to brown the fruited side. Serve warm and buttered.

VANILLA WAFFLES

Preheat the oven to 60°C. Preheat your waffle maker.

Follow the recipe for American Pancakes adding 1 teaspoon of vanilla essence into the batter.

Pour sufficient batter into the waffle maker to fill the moulds, and cook until the waffles are golden brown and release from the mould.

Lift into an ovenproof dish and keep warm in the oven while you make the rest.

**Making these pancakes at weekends has become a favourite family ritual at home because the process involves us all and is conducive to a rare slow start to the day. This recipe also makes great waffles. Serve on warm plates simply dredged with icing sugar, a delicious topping of your choice (see opposite), or with sliced banana, fresh berries and/or maple syrup and Greek yoghurt.**

Preheat the oven to 60°C.

To prepare the pancakes, sift the flours, ground almonds, baking powder and salt into a medium bowl.

Beat the egg yolks together, and whisk in the milk.

Make a large well in the centre of the flour mixture, and pour in a third of the egg and milk mixture.

To incorporate the flour, stir the egg and milk mixture in small circles with a wooden spoon, so that the flour is slowly drawn from the sides of the well into the liquid. Do not stir vigorously, or the flour will not be mixed evenly, resulting in a lumpy batter. Once the mixture in the well is smooth, add more of the milk, continuing to stir in small circles and slowly drawing in the flour mixture, until all the milk has been added, the dry ingredients are incorporated and the batter is smooth and thick.

In a separate, clean bowl, whisk the egg whites until they hold their shape but wobble when shaken. Stir a large spoonful of the egg whites into the pancake batter. Gently fold through the remaining egg whites, to form a light and airy batter.

Lightly grease the pan with oil, and place over a high heat. Once the oil starts to smoke, pour enough of the batter into the centre of the pan to form a pancake about 12.5 cm across. Cook undisturbed until bubbles form on the surface and the bottom is golden brown and released from the pan. Turn over with a fish slice, and continue to cook until the pancake has puffed up and feels springy in the centre. Keep warm under foil in the oven while you prepare the remaining pancakes in the same way.

## CARAMELISED CINNAMON APPLES

**These golden apples make the perfect filling for freshly made crêpes and an ideal topping for American pancakes and waffles.**

**SERVES 4**

- 85 g granulated sugar
- 85 g unsalted butter or dairy-free margarine
- 4 Granny Smith apples, peeled, cored and thickly sliced
- 1 tsp ground cinnamon

Place the granulated sugar and 1 tablespoon water in a frying pan over a medium heat. Swirl the pan slowly until the sugar has dissolved. Continue to cook until the sugar caramelises to a rich golden brown colour. Turn off the heat and carefully stir in the butter to make the caramel sauce.

Stir the sliced apples and cinnamon into the caramel, and gently simmer over a low heat for 10–15 minutes, until the apples are tender and golden brown.

Remove from the heat and serve warm.

## SPICED BLUEBERRY COMPOTE

**This aromatic and richly coloured compote is delicious hot or cold, spooned over hot pancakes, waffles, crêpes, French toast and Greek yoghurt. A perfect partner for ice cream and cheesecake too.**

**SERVES 4**

- 250 g blueberries
- 100 g caster sugar
- 1 vanilla pod, split lengthways
- 2 strips each of lemon zest and orange zest
- juice of ½ lemon
- 1 cinnamon stick

Place all the ingredients in a medium pan over a heat and simmer for 8 minutes, stirring occasionally.

Remove and discard the cinnamon stick, vanilla pod and strips of zest, and continue to cook before serving hot or at room temperature.

*Tip*

**Make sure that you start to cook the pancakes as soon as the batter is made, to make the most of the bubbles produced by the baking powder.**

# BRETON BUCKWHEAT CRÊPES

• SERVES 4 – MAKES 6 LARGE OR 8 MEDIUM

110 g buckwheat flour
1 tsp ground cinnamon
1 tbsp caster sugar
½ tsp salt
300 ml milk or dairy-free milk
2 medium eggs, beaten
sunflower oil for cooking

**This recipe is for Yann Salaun, my Breton colleague, who has a passion for the benefits of buckwheat. These delicate but wholesome crêpes are delicious spread with Nutella, drizzled with lemon juice and sugar, or, for a more indulgent filling, served with Caramelised Cinnamon Apples or Spiced Blueberry Compote (page 25).**

Preheat the oven to 60°C.

To prepare the crêpes, sift the flour, cinnamon, sugar and salt into a medium bowl. In a separate bowl, whisk the milk into the eggs.

Make a large well in the centre of the sifted flour, and pour in a third of the egg and milk mixture.

To incorporate the flour mixture, stir the egg and milk in small circles with a wooden spoon, so that the flour is slowly drawn from the sides of the well into the liquid. Do not stir vigorously, or the flour will not be evenly mixed, resulting in a lumpy batter.

Once the mixture in the well is smooth, gradually pour in the remaining egg and milk mixture and continue to stir in small circles, until all the dry ingredients are incorporated and the batter is smooth.

Lightly grease the pan with oil, and place over a high heat. Once the oil starts to smoke, pour the batter into the centre of the pan and swirl around the pan until the bottom of the pan is covered. Leave the pancake to cook until it forms bubbles on the surface and releases from the pan.

Flip the pancake over with a fish slice, and cook for a further 30 seconds, or until it is golden brown and releases from the pan.

Continue making the pancakes in the same way until all the batter has been used, stacking the pancakes on a large plate as you go and keeping warm under foil in the oven.

Serve on warmed plates, flat or rolled with toppings of your choice.

# HASH BROWN WITH ONION & BACON

**This crispy potato cake is delicious served with a fried egg and roasted vine tomatoes for a Sunday breakfast, or serve as part of a main meal with fish or poultry. Use floury potatoes such as King Edwards or Maris Pipers, to make a hash brown with a fluffy interior and crispy shell.**

- SERVES 4

3 tbsp sunflower oil, for frying, if needed
4 streaky bacon rashers, sliced across into thin lardons
1 large onion, finely diced
4 large floury potatoes, peeled
salt and freshly ground black pepper

Heat the oil in a large frying pan over a medium heat. Add the bacon and fry until golden brown. With a slotter spoon, lift the bacon out of the pan and set aside. Reduce the heat to low, keeping the bacon fat in the pan. Add the onion and soften over a low heat for 10 minutes. Add to the bacon with a slotted spoon.

Meanwhile, peel and coarsely grate the potatoes. Place in the centre of a clean tea towel and twist the ends as tightly as you can to squeeze the liquid out of the potatoes. Transfer the potato to a medium bowl.

Stir bacon and onion mixture into the grated potato, and season with salt and pepper.

Return the pan to a high heat, adding 1 tablespoon of oil to the bacon fat if needed. When the fat is hot but not smoking, pour in the potato mixture and flatten over the base of the pan with a fish slice. Reduce the heat to medium-low.

Gently fry the potato cake for 3–5 minutes until the underside is golden brown and sufficiently crispy to loosen itself from the pan.

Remove the pan from the heat, and cover with a flat baking sheet. Wearing oven gloves, flip the pan over so that the hash brown is resting on the baking sheet, browned side up. Return the pan to the heat and heat the remaining 1 tablespoon of oil. Slide the hash brown back into the pan and brown the second side for 2–3 minutes until golden brown and crisp.

With a sharp knife, cut the hash brown cake into quarters, and serve immediately with fried eggs and roasted vine tomatoes.

# PIPERADE

- SERVES 4

3–4 tbsp olive oil
60 g gluten-free chorizo sausage, outer casing removed, thinly sliced
1 large onion, diced
1 large red pepper, deseeded and diced
1 large green pepper, deseeded and diced
2 large tomatoes, peeled, deseeded and diced
2 garlic cloves, finely chopped
1 small red chilli, deseeded and membrane removed, finely chopped (optional)
8 large eggs, lightly beaten
4 slices brown or white gluten-free bread
salt and freshly ground black pepper

**This Basque-inspired dish is a colourful, flavoursome and interesting way to enjoy scrambled eggs. Ideal for brunch or a light meal.**

Heat 2 tablespoons of olive oil in a large, heavy frying pan over a medium heat.

Fry the chorizo, onions and peppers gently for 10 minutes, or until the vegetables have softened.

Add the tomatoes, garlic and chilli (if using), and fry until warmed through.

Season the beaten eggs with salt and pepper, and slowly stir into the vegetables, loosely scrambling the egg to your desired firmness.

Toast the bread and generously butter or drizzle with olive oil. Arrange on four plates, top with a generous spoonful of Basque Scrambled Eggs and serve immediately.

# ENGLISH MUFFINS WITH SPINACH, SCRAMBLED EGG & SMOKED SALMON

• SERVES 4

• FOR THE WILTED SPINACH

15 g butter or 1 tbsp light olive oil
2 large handfuls of washed and dried young spinach leaves
pinch of salt and freshly ground black pepper
pinch of freshly grated nutmeg

• FOR THE SCRAMBLED EGG

15 g butter or 1 tbsp vegetable oil
6 medium eggs, beaten
salt and freshly ground black pepper

• TO SERVE

4 gluten-free English muffins
4 large slices smoked salmon
4 grinds of black pepper
1 tbsp finely sliced chives
4 lemon wedges

**A special breakfast for a lazy Sunday morning with the papers.**

First, wilt the spinach. Gently melt the butter or heat the oil over a low heat and add the spinach, salt, pepper and nutmeg to the pan. Stir continuously until the spinach is just wilted. With a slotted spoon, remove the spinach and set aside.

To make the scambled egg, pour any liquid out of the pan and gently melt the butter or heat the oil. Season the beaten eggs with salt and pepper, and pour into the pan. Slowly stir the eggs for 3 minutes, or until the eggs are almost set or form large soft lumps. Stir in the reserved spinach, and continue to cook until the eggs are softly set.

Spoon the eggs and spinach onto toasted and buttered English muffins. Top each serving with a slice of smoked salmon, a grind of pepper, a sprinkling of chives and a wedge of lemon.

# HAM, TOMATO & CHEESE-FILLED CROISSANTS

• SERVES 4

4 gluten-free croissants
4 slices good-quality ham
2 ripe vine tomatoes, thinly sliced
4 large slices Gruyère, Emmental or medium Cheddar
freshly ground black pepper

**Perfect for a late weekend breakfast or light meal with salad.**

Preheat the oven to 180°C.

Using a bread knife, slice the croissants lengthways through the middle.

Place a ham slice in each, followed by the evenly divided tomato slices and a slice of cheese. Season with black pepper.

Place the filled croissants on a baking sheet, and bake in the oven until the cheese has melted and the croissant is crisp and warmed through.

# FRUITY FRENCH CINNAMON TOAST

**Try this sweet, aromatic and more refined cousin of eggy bread for a treat at weekends with summer berries, honey and sliced banana, or with homemade Spiced Blueberry Compote (page 25) and Greek yoghurt. For a simpler tasting version, replace fruit loaf with white or brown gluten-free bread.**

Preheat the oven to 60°C.

In a shallow dish, whisk the eggs, milk, honey and cinnamon together.

Turn the bread over in the egg mixture and leave to soak for 2 minutes.

Heat the oil in a frying pan, then fry the eggy bread, a few slices at a time, until golden brown. Place in the oven to keep warm.

Dredge the warm French toast with the cinnamon-flavoured icing sugar.

Stack 3 pieces of French toast on warmed plates. Serve immediately.

- SERVES 4

2 medium eggs, beaten
150 ml milk or dairy-free milk
1 tbsp runny honey
½ tsp ground cinnamon
6 slices gluten-free fruit loaf, sliced in half diagonally
2 tbsp oil or 30 g unsalted butter for shallow-frying
1 tbsp icing sugar mixed with 1 tsp ground cinnamon

# TURKISH EGGS ON TOAST

**A delicious brunch dish to remind you of the sun at any time of year – and an interesting way to serve fried eggs.**

Preheat the oven to 200°C.

Brush both sides of each slice of bread with olive oil, and season with salt and pepper. Bake in the oven for 5–10 minutes, until golden brown.

Meanwhile, heat 1 tablespoon of oil in a non-stick frying pan over a medium heat. Add the onion, garlic, cumin and chilli flakes, and season with salt and pepper. Gently fry until soft. Remove from the pan with a slotted spoon, set aside and mix in the lemon juice.

Return the pan to the heat and add another tablespoon of olive oil. Fry the eggs until the whites are set but the yolks are still runny.

Place the toast slices on a serving dish, dollop a dessertspoon of yoghurt onto each slice of toast, then top with the spicy fried onions, followed by the eggs. Sprinkle with mint and serve immediately.

- SERVES 4

4 slices gluten-free white bread
2–3 tbsp extra virgin olive oil
1 large red onion, thinly sliced
1 garlic clove, finely chopped
1 tsp cumin seeds
pinch of red chilli flakes
juice of 1 lemon
4 large eggs
250 ml Greek yoghurt or dairy-free, unsweetened natural yoghurt
2 tbsp roughly chopped fresh mint
salt and freshly ground black pepper

# CORN FRITTERS WITH AVOCADO SALSA, SOUR CREAM & CRISPY BACON

**A hearty start to the day, this recipe is inspired by a happy New Year's Day brunch in the sun with my family at Bronte Beach, Sydney.**

Preheat the oven to 80°C.

Place the drained sweetcorn in a medium bowl and mix with the spring onions, chilli (if using) and coriander. Set aside.

Sift both flours, baking powder and 1 teaspoon salt into a separate bowl. Crack the eggs into a jug and add the milk. Whisk until well combined.

Make a well in the centre of the dry ingredients. Gradually pour the egg mixture into the well, whisking continuously until the batter is smooth.

Stir in the reserved corn mixture, and season with salt and pepper. Leave the batter to rest for 10 minutes.

Meanwhile, mix all the salsa ingredients together in a bowl, then cover and set aside.

To cook the fritters, heat 1 tablespoon of vegetable oil in a large frying pan over a medium heat. Drop a heaped tablespoon of the corn batter into the pan and gently fry for 2 minutes on each side, or until the fritters are golden brown and crisp. Transfer to a plate lined with baking paper and keep warm in the oven while you prepare the remaining fritters.

Fry the bacon until crisp and golden.

To serve, layer 2 or 3 corn fritters with soured cream and avocado salsa. Arrange 2 crispy bacon rashers on the top of each serving and serve immediately with lime wedges.

• SERVES 4 – MAKES 8–10

230 g tinned sweetcorn kernels, drained
4 spring onions, finely sliced
handful of coriander leaves, finely chopped
1 small red chilli, deseeded, membrane removed, finely diced (optional)
80 g cornflour
80 g rice flour
1 tsp salt
½ tsp baking powder
3 medium eggs, beaten
100 ml milk or dairy-free milk
salt and freshly ground black pepper
vegetable oil for frying

• FOR THE AVOCADO, CORIANDER AND TOMATO SALSA

1 large avocado, peeled, stoned and diced
2 ripe vine tomatoes, diced
2 garlic cloves, finely chopped
zest and juice of 1 lime
1 tsp caster sugar
handful of chopped coriander
2 tbsp vegetable oil
salt and freshly ground black pepper, to taste

• FOR THE GARNISH

8 streaky bacon rashers
soured cream, optional
lime wedges, to serve

# SPANISH POTATO & ONION TORTILLA

• SERVES 6–8

- 600 g small waxy potatoes, such as Désirée, Vivaldi or Charlotte, peeled and thinly sliced
- 2 large Spanish onions, thinly sliced
- 200 ml extra virgin olive oil
- 10 large eggs, lightly beaten
- salt and freshly ground black pepper

*Tip*

**Tortilla makes a welcome change to a sandwich for lunch on the go.**

**I have enjoyed this traditional Spanish breakfast many times, in an old convent hotel in the Cantabrian mountains. In Spain, tortilla is often made the night before, and served for breakfast the following morning, cold or gently warmed. For a true Spanish experience, serve with thinly sliced Iberico ham and toast rubbed with garlic and ripe tomatoes, then drizzled with extra virgin olive oil. Use a large ovenproof non-stick or well-seasoned frying pan with a lid, measuring 30 cm across.**

Mix the sliced potatoes and onions together with half the oil, a large pinch of salt and 3 or 4 grinds of pepper.

Heat the frying pan over a medium heat, and pour in the potato mixture. Reduce the heat to low and cover the pan with a lid. Cook gently, stirring regularly, for 20–30 minutes until the potatoes and onions are soft but not coloured.

Season the beaten eggs with a large pinch of salt and pepper, and stir the cooked potato mixture into them, being careful not to break up the potatoes.

Clean the frying pan thoroughly, then heat the remaining oil and pour in the egg and potato mixture. Over a low heat, gently cook the tortilla for 20–30 minutes, without stirring, until the egg is set in the centre.

Heat the grill and brown the top of the tortilla for 2 minutes, or until golden brown.

To turn the tortilla out of the pan, first loosen the sides and base with a palette knife and carefully pour off any hot oil. Over the kitchen sink, place a large serving plate over the rim of the pan. Using oven gloves to protect your hands, flip the pan upside down. Lower the plate on to the work surface. Give the base of the pan a few sharp raps and ease the pan away from the tortilla, being careful to loosen any sticking potatoes.

To serve, eat hot or at room temperature cut into generous slices.

# SPICED BUTTERNUT SQUASH, BACON, GOAT'S CHEESE & MAPLE SYRUP TART

**This rich and tasty sweet and salty tart makes a special brunch dish served with Greek yoghurt or a light meal with salad.**

- SERVES 4

500 g butternut squash, peeled, deseeded and cut into 1-cm cubes
1 tbsp olive oil
½ tsp ground cinnamon
½ tsp chilli flakes
2 tbsp maple syrup
1 x 400g pack gluten-free puff pastry, defrosted
12 good-quality smoked streaky bacon rashers
150 g goat's cheese, cut into dice (optional)
salt and freshly ground black pepper

Preheat the oven to 200°C.

Spread out the diced butternut squash in a single layer in a baking dish. Drizzle with the olive oil and season with salt and pepper. Bake for 20 minutes, or until the butternut squash is very soft, then leave to cool.

Pour the cooled butternut squash into a bowl, add the cinnamon, chilli flakes and 1 tablespoon of the maple syrup, and mash to a smooth purée.

Roll out the puff pastry to a rectangle 20 cm x 30 cm. Trim away the edges with a sharp knife, and place the pastry on a baking sheet. Prick all over with a fork, leaving a 2-cm border around the edge. Spread the butternut purée evenly over the pastry base, leaving the border clear.

Cover the butternut purée with overlapping bacon rashers arranged across the tart, and sprinkle over the goat's cheese (if using). Drizzle with the remaining maple syrup, and bake for 20 minutes, or until the bacon is golden and crisp, and the puff pastry base is cooked and golden brown in the centre. To check the base, gently lift the corner of the tart with a fish slice and look underneath.

Serve hot with a spoonful of yoghurt on the side.

# ENGLISH BREAKFAST PUFF PASTRY TULIPS WITH GRUYÈRE & DIJON GRATIN

- SERVES 4

- FOR PASTRY CASES

1 x 400g pack gluten-free puff pastry, defrosted
1 medium egg, beaten

- FOR THE FILLING

1 tbsp olive oil
2 smoked streaky bacon rashers, very thinly sliced
½ small onion, thinly sliced
40 g button mushrooms, thinly sliced
2 tsp chopped flat-leaf parsley
4 small eggs
4 tbsp double cream
1 tsp Dijon mustard
20 g Gruyère cheese, grated
salt and freshly ground black pepper

- TO SERVE

1 tbsp Gruyère cheese, finely grated
1 tbsp finely chopped flat-leaf parsley
18 tomatoes on the vine, cut into groups of 3

**Serve these attractive puff pastry tulips for a special breakfast or brunch with roast cherry tomatoes on the vine or a green salad.**

Preheat the oven to 200°C.

To make the pastry cases, roll out the pastry into a large square 2 mm thick. With a sharp knife, trim the edges of the pastry and cut into 4 squares.

Ease each pastry square into a hole in a 12-hole large muffin tin. Press the pastry against the base and sides of each hole, and bend the edges of the pastry outwards to form open tulip shapes.

Scrunch up 4 squares of greaseproof paper, then flatten out and line each of the tartlets. Pour rice grains into each lined pastry tulip to a depth of 1 cm. Bake the tulips for 10–15 minutes until the pastry is light golden and firm. Carefully remove the paper and rice, and return the tulips to the oven for a further 5 minutes, or until the base of the pastry is golden brown.

Brush the inside of each baked tulip case with a little beaten egg, and return to the oven for a further minute to set. Set aside the remaining egg for the Gruyère topping. Remove the tulip cases from the oven, set aside and leave to cool in the muffin tin.

Reduce the oven temperature to 180°C.

To make the filling, fry the bacon lardons in the olive oil until golden brown, and lift onto a dish with a slotted spoon. Add the onion and mushrooms to the same pan, season with salt and pepper, and gently fry until soft. Stir in the parsley and fried bacon and spoon into the tulip cases.

Crack an egg into each filled tulip, being careful not to break the yolks.

Mix the cream with the Dijon mustard, Gruyère cheese, the remaining beaten egg and a grind of pepper, and spoon into each tulip to the rim.

Sprinkle the filled tulips with Gruyère cheese and bake – along with the vine tomatoes in a separate dish – for 15–20 minutes. The tulips are ready when the cream mixture is puffed and golden brown.

To serve, place a tulip and three roast tomatoes on 4 warmed plates.

INOX-NOGENT ★★★

# PORRIDGE WITH HONEY, FLAKED ALMONDS, MEDJOOL DATES & BANANA

- SERVES 4

8 Medjool dates, pitted and cut into quarters lengthways
40 g flaked almonds, toasted
200 g gluten-free, rolled oats
800 ml milk or dairy-free milk
runny honey
2 bananas, peeled and sliced on the diagonal

**Porridge is the perfect start to the day, particularly on cold winter mornings. This traditional Scottish staple is transformed into an indulgent, rather exotic breakfast with the addition of succulent dates and crunchy toasted almonds.**

Mix the dates and almonds together.

In a medium pan, bring the oats and milk to the boil, and simmer for 5 minutes, stirring continuously until thickened.

Remove from the heat and spoon into 4 serving bowls.

To serve, drizzle 1 dessertspoon of runny honey over each bowl of porridge. Top with sliced banana, cut on the diagonal, and sprinkle on the dates and flaked almonds.

*Tip*

**For a simpler breakfast, top the porridge with sliced banana and maple syrup or a spoonful of Muscovado sugar. If you cannot eat oats, replace them with a half-and-half mix of rice and quinoa flakes, and simmer the milk for 10 minutes until soft.**

# APPLE & BERRY BIRCHER MUESLI

**A really convenient and nourishing breakfast that is best made the night before and stored in the fridge for up to 2 days. Experiment with the combination of seeds, nuts and fruit.**

• SERVES 4

200 g gluten-free rolled porridge oats
200 ml semi-skimmed milk, almond milk or coconut milk
80 ml apple juice
400 g fruit yoghurt or dairy-free yoghurt of your choice
2 large Granny Smith apples, peeled, cored and grated
20 g sunflower seeds
20 g flaxseed
20 g pumpkin seeds
50 g flaked almonds
50 g dried cranberries, sultanas, chopped dates or apricots

• TOPPING

200 g fresh blueberries, blackberries or raspberries, or a mixture of all three
handful of mixed seeds
flaked almonds
honey or maple syrup, for drizzling

Mix the oats, milk, apple juice, 200g of the yoghurt, grated apple, seeds, nuts and dried fruit together in a bowl then store in airtight container in the fridge overnight.

To serve, divide the bircher muesli between 4 cereal bowls, and top with the remaining yoghurt. Scatter over the blueberries, mixed seeds, flaked almonds and a drizzle of honey or maple syrup.

# SEED, FRUIT & NUT GRANOLA

• MAKES ABOUT 1.2 KG

50 g sunflower oil
3 tbsp runny honey
3 tbsp maple syrup
1 tsp ground cinnamon
pinch of salt
300 g gluten-free rolled oats
150 g hazelnuts, roughly chopped
150 g flaked almonds
75 g sunflower seeds
75 g pumpkin seeds
1 tbsp flaxseed
1 tbsp chia seeds
50 g raisins
50 g sultanas
75 g chopped dates
100 g dried apricots, sliced
50 g banana chips
25 g freeze-dried strawberries

**This crunchy, chewy, nutritious granola will keep you satisfied until lunchtime. Carry as a snack to nibble on while you are out and about. Pair with Greek yoghurt, fresh fruit or Spiced Blueberry Compote (page 25).**

Preheat the oven to 170°C, and line a baking sheet with greaseproof paper.

In a pan, bring the oil, honey, maple syrup and 2 tablespoons of water to a simmer, stirring all the time until smooth and well combined. Stir in the cinnamon and salt. Remove from the heat.

Mix the oats, nuts and seeds together in a large bowl, then stir in the hot honey mixture until the dry ingredients are thoroughly coated.

Spread out the mixture over the lined baking sheet, and bake in the oven for 30 minutes. Turn the granola over with a fish slice, reduce the oven temperature to 150°C and continue to bake the granola for a further 30 minutes, or until the oat and nut mixture is golden and crunchy. Remove from the oven and immediately mix with the dried fruit, being careful not to break up the baked granola clusters. Leave to cool.

Store in an airtight container for up to 2 weeks.

*Tip*

**For variation, replace the hazelnuts with pistachios or pecans, and use dried cranberries and blueberries in place of the dates and banana chips. If oats are out of bounds, use quinoa flakes or puffed rice instead.**

# Starters, Light Meals & Party Food

Including delicious morsels such as bruschetta and spiced pitta chips, soups including gazpacho and salads made with quinoa, this chapter offers fabulous ideas for light meals to be shared with friends and family.

# BRUSCHETTA, CROUTES & CROSTINI

**While I was resident cook at an idyllic Tuscan farmhouse, I regularly made these to serve with pre-dinner drinks. All who tried them gave them a thumbs up! Obviously, they are equally good when made with gluten-free bread.**

## BRUSCHETTA

In its simplest form, *bruschetta* is the name given to thick slices of toasted bread, rubbed with garlic and sometimes ½ a ripe tomato, then drizzled with olive oil. It is the most delicious, purest form of snack I know. Bruschetta is perfect for serving with pre-dinner drinks and informal starters, or topped with the recipes below and opposite.

### MAKES SIMPLE BRUSCHETTA FOR 4 PEOPLE

Take 4 gluten-free white rolls and slice into 1-cm pieces, then toast. Rub the cut side with a peeled garlic clove and ½ a ripe tomato (if you like), then drizzle with extra virgin olive oil and lightly season with salt.

## CROUTES AND CROSTINI

Croutes, and the Italian equivalent crostini, are made by thinly slicing a flute-shaped artisanal bread such as a baguette or using a pastry cutter to cut bite-sized shapes from slices of white bread. These are then drizzled with olive oil and baked until crisp and golden.

They are topped with a wide variety of savoury toppings, both rustic and refined, usually to serve as canapés with drinks before a meal.

### MAKES CROUTES FOR 4 PEOPLE

Preheat the oven to 200°C.

With a sharp bread knife, cut 20 slices, no more than 1 cm thick, from a gluten-free baguette. Spread out the slices over the bottom of a large, shallow baking tin.

Brush both sides of each croute with melted unsalted butter or extra virgin olive oil. Season lightly with salt, and bake for 8–10 minutes until the croutes are golden brown on both sides.

Transfer the croutes to a wire rack to cool. Use as required or store in an airtight container for up to 3 days. Refresh in a hot oven for 2 minutes before using to revive their crunch.

## STEAMED ASPARAGUS WITH PROSCIUTTO & PARMESAN SHAVINGS

**The complex saltiness of prosciutto and Parmesan pairs beautifully with vivid-green, tender asparagus.**

### MAKES 8 BRUSCHETTA

- 16 slender, fresh asparagus tips, cut to 5 cm long, steamed until al dente
- 1 tbsp extra virgin olive oil
- 8 thin prosciutto slices
- 8 freshly prepared bruschetta toasts (see above)
- 50 g Parmesan, thinly shaved from the block with a potato peeler
- salt and freshly ground black pepper

In a bowl, gently toss the asparagus tips with the olive oil, and season with salt and pepper.

Arrange a slice of prosciutto on each bruschetta, and top each one with two asparagus spears. Sprinkle with Parmesan shavings, and serve immediately.

## ROASTED PEPPERS WITH ANCHOVIES & CAPERS

**Roasting the peppers sweetens their flavour, delicious with rich and salty anchovies, the sharpness of capers and aromatic basil.**

MAKES 8 BRUSCHETTA

- 2 red peppers
- 2 anchovies, drained and finely chopped
- 1 tsp small capers, rinsed and drained
- 1 tbsp finely sliced basil
- 8 freshly prepared bruschetta (see opposite)
- salt and freshly ground black pepper

Heat the grill to high and blacken the skin of the peppers on all sides.

Transfer the peppers to a bowl, cover with cling film and leave to steam for 15 minutes to loosen the skin.

Remove the cling film, and peel the peppers using a small, sharp knife, discarding the skin. Core and deseed the peeled peppers, then slice thinly lengthways.

Place the sliced pepper in a small, clean bowl, and mix in the anchovies and capers. Season judiciously with salt and pepper, bearing in mind the saltiness of the capers and anchovies.

Stir in the basil, then heap the mixture onto the warm bruschetta and serve immediately.

## ROASTED FENNEL, COURGETTE & MINT

**The delicate aniseed flavour of the fennel and sweetness in the courgette are brought to the fore with roasting, especially when mixed with lemon and mint. These bruschetta look beautiful too.**

MAKES 8 BRUSCHETTA

- 1 medium courgette, sliced into long ribbons with a potato peeler
- 1 fennel bulb, thinly sliced lengthways with a sharp knife or mandolin
- 4 tbsp extra virgin olive oil
- juice of 1 small lemon
- 1 heaped tbsp chopped mint
- 8 freshly prepared bruschetta toasts (see opposite)
- salt and freshly ground black pepper

Preheat the oven to 200°C.

Place the courgette and fennel on a baking sheet. Drizzle with half the olive oil, and season with salt and pepper. Bake in the oven for 10 minutes, or until turning golden brown around the edges. Place in a mixing bowl.

Toss with the lemon juice, the remaining olive oil and mint. Check seasoning. Pile on to the freshly prepared bruschetta and serve immediately.

## FRESH FIGS WITH MASCARPONE & WILD ROCKET

**The flavour and colour of figs are at their richest in early or late summer, depending on the variety. Their aromatic, fresh flavour pairs beautifully with creamy mascarpone, made all the more vibrant with peppery rocket and a hint of balsamic vinegar.**

MAKES 8 BRUSCHETTA

- 2 tsp balsamic vinegar
- 1 tbsp extra virgin olive oil
- 2 large ripe figs, cut into eighths
- 8 freshly prepared bruschetta toasts (see opposite)
- 200 g mascarpone
- 40 g wild rocket
- salt and freshly ground black pepper

Put the balsamic vinegar in a small bowl. Season with salt and pepper, then whisk in the oil.

Coat the fig pieces in the dressing.

Thickly spread the bruschetta with mascarpone, and top with the rocket leaves and dressed figs.

Serve immediately.

# CHICKEN CAESAR SALAD

- SERVES 4

2 skinless boneless chicken breasts
1 tablespoon light olive oil
1 large cos or romaine lettuce, leaves separated, rinsed in cold water and spun dry
8 salted anchovy fillets, halved lengthways

- FOR THE DRESSING

3 salted anchovy fillets
110 g Parmesan, finely grated
1 garlic clove, finely chopped
5 tbsp good-quality mayonnaise (check the label for gluten)
1 tbsp white wine vinegar
salt and freshly ground black pepper
50 g Parmesan shavings, to garnish

- FOR THE CROUTONS

4 slices gluten-free white bread, cut into 1.5-cm cubes
3 tbsp light olive oil
salt

**This globally-loved salad is a safe bet even for family and friends who don't usually enjoy salad. Delicious served with or without the chicken.**

Make the croutons, following the instructions opposite.

Season the chicken breasts with salt and pepper. Gently fry in the olive oil for 4 minutes on each side, or until the centre of the breasts are no longer pink and juices run clear when tested with a sharp knife. Remove from the pan and set aside. Retain any chicken juices in the pan for the dressing.

To make the Caesar dressing, mash the anchovies against the side of a small bowl with a fork. Mix in the remaining dressing ingredients and chicken juices, then season with salt and pepper. The dressing should be the consistency of double cream. If it is too thick, gradually stir in 1–2 dessertspoons of water until you have achieved the required consistency.

To make the salad, tear the lettuce into bite-sized pieces, and place in a salad bowl. Pull the warm chicken into bite-sized strips, and scatter half of it over the leaves, along with half the croutons. Pour in two-thirds of the dressing, and toss the salad with your fingers.

Scatter over the remaining chicken, croutons and anchovy fillets, then drizzle over the remaining dressing and sprinkle with Parmesan shavings. Serve immediately.

## CROUTONS

**Croutons add crunch and colour, sprinkled onto soups and salads. Garnish smooth, delicate soups with croutons cut no larger than 1 cm wide. Rustic soups and salads require larger, more irregular croutons of 1.5–2.5 cm wide, to enhance the appearance and add robust crunch to the dish. Use plain olive oil or butter to cook all-purpose croutons. For more flavour and colour, replace the plain oil with chilli, or garlic-flavoured oil, and try tossing the croutons in chopped rosemary, finely grated Parmesan or ground spices before baking.**

MAKES CROUTONS FOR 4 PEOPLE

Preheat the oven to 200°C.

Remove the crusts from 4 slices of gluten-free white sandwich bread, and cut into even-sized cubes 1 cm wide. For rustic croutons, dice artisanal gluten-free white or brown loaf or rolls into cubes 2–2.5 cm wide.

Spread the cubes of bread over the bottom of a large shallow roasting dish, and drizzle over 2 tablespoons of plain or flavoured oil. Toss the cubes of bread in the oil (and other flavouring ingredients such as 1 tablespoon of grated Parmesan or chopped rosemary or thyme leaves) and lightly season with salt.

Bake for 8–10 minutes, turning the croutons a few times during cooking until crisp and golden.

Sprinkle the freshly made hot croutons onto soups and salads, or pour the croutons into a large, shallow tray covered with absorbent kitchen paper to cool.

Croutons can be stored in an airtight container for up to 3 days. Refresh in a hot oven for 2–3 minutes before serving.

# FRENCH ONION SOUP WITH GRUYÈRE & DIJON MUSTARD CROUTES

**A warming, richly flavoured soup perfect for winter, thanks to the slow-cooked onions topped with a melting cheesy croute.**

- SERVES 4

55 g butter
450 g onions, thinly sliced
1 garlic clove, crushed
1 tsp cornflour
1.1 litres strong fresh chicken stock
55 g Gruyère cheese, grated
4 tsp Dijon mustard
4 slices gluten-free baguette or large rounds cut out of gluten-free sliced white bread with a pastry cutter
salt and freshly ground black pepper

Melt the butter in a large casserole dish. Stir in the onions and season with salt and pepper. Cover with a lid and fry slowly, stirring regularly until very soft and caramel brown. This will take about 40 minutes.

Stir in the garlic, and fry for 30 seconds. Stir in the cornflour. Pour over the chicken stock, then simmer for 20 minutes. Pour the soup into 4 individual ovenproof bowls and place them on a baking tray.

Preheat the oven to 200°C.

Mix the cheese with the Dijon mustard and three grinds of black pepper.

Spread the cheese mixture on to the bread, then place each slice on the surface of the soup, with the cheese topping uppermost.

Bake the soup in the preheated oven for 10 minutes, or until the croutes are well browned and the soup is bubbling. Serve immediately.

# PANZANELLA

**This refreshing and moreish salad, based on bread, tastes most vibrant in the summer months when made with perfectly ripe tomatoes, peppers and fresh basil.**

With a fork, mash the garlic, anchovies and capers to a purée on a chopping board, and place in the bottom of a salad bowl.

Add the diced pepper and red onion to the anchovy purée, and stir in the olive oil and vinegar. Cover and chill for 15 minutes.

Place the toasted bread squares in a separate bowl. Mash half of the diced tomatoes and mix through the bread. Leave for 15 minutes to allow the bread to soak up the juices.

Add the remaining diced tomatoes and cucumber to the peppers and anchovy mixture. Stir in the soaked bread and shredded basil. Taste and season with salt and pepper.

Serve with green salad and grilled or barbecued meat.

• SERVES 4

1 garlic clove, finely chopped
4 anchovy fillets, rinsed and finely chopped
1 tbsp capers, rinsed and finely chopped
1 red pepper, deseeded and diced
1 small red onion, thinly sliced
4 tbsp extra virgin olive oil
1 tbsp red wine vinegar
4 slices gluten-free white bread, toasted and cut into 2-cm squares
4 ripe tomatoes, skinned and diced
½ cucumber, peeled, deseeded and diced
½ bunch of fresh basil, shredded
salt and freshly ground black pepper

*Tip*

**Make the most of the tender flesh of tomatoes by removing the skin. To skin tomatoes, plunge them into simmering water for 8 seconds – no longer, or the flesh will become mushy. With a slotted spoon, transfer the tomatoes to a bowl of cold water. After 2 minutes, pour away the water and refill with fresh cold water to cool the tomatoes quickly. When the tomatoes are completely cold, peel off the skin with a sharp knife. Use as required.**

# BREADCRUMBS

**Breadcrumbs are enormously versatile in cooking, creating a crunchy, golden coating and a crisp crust on baked dishes. They also thicken rustic soups and can be added to stuffing and dishes made with minced meat, as they help to bind mixtures together and hold on to the cooking juices and flavour.**

## BREADCRUMBS FOR COATING FOOD

Lean, tender meats and delicate fish can be kept soft and succulent – and given contrasting crunch – when protected by a crisp coating of crumbs. Use finely crumbed bread for formal dishes and coarser breadcrumbs for rustic dishes.

**TO COAT 450 G OF FISH, POULTRY OR MEAT, TO SERVE 4**

- 2 tbsp rice flour or cornflour, seasoned with salt and pepper
- 2 eggs, beaten
- 225 g gluten-free white bread, crusts removed and whizzed into coarse or fine breadcrumbs

Place the flour, eggs and breadcrumbs separately in each of three wide, shallow dishes. Thinly coat the meat or fish in the seasoned flour, shaking off any excess. Dip the floured pieces into the beaten egg. Transfer the flour-and-egged food to the dish of breadcrumbs and coat thoroughly and evenly. Shallow-fry, deep-fry or bake as needed.

## BREADCRUMB ALTERNATIVES

Wholesome alternatives to breadcrumbs for coating food include:

- ground almonds, hazelnuts or pistachio nuts
- sesame seeds
- gluten-free oats, coarse polenta or crushed plain or salted popcorn
- finely grated potato or parsnip for a rough, crisp coating

## BREADCRUMB SPRINKLES

To add crunch and golden colour to a baked dish, or to meat or fish, serving 4 people mix 4 tablespoons of fine or coarse breadcrumbs or one of the crumb alternatives listed below left, with any one of the following:

- 1 finely chopped garlic clove, ½ tsp red chilli flakes, a pinch of salt and ground black pepper
- 2 tbsp finely grated Parmesan, a pinch of salt and freshly ground black pepper
- 1 finely chopped garlic clove, grated zest of 1 lemon, 1 tbps of chopped fresh thyme or rosemary, a pinch of salt and ground black pepper
- 2 tsp gluten-free spice seasonings such as piri piri, ras el hanout or Cajun spice, a pinch of salt and ground black pepper

Sprinkle the flavoured breadcrumbs over the baked dish or over meat or fish portions placed side by side in a large ovenproof dish. Bake in a preheated 180°–200°C oven for the time given in the recipe, or until the crust is golden and crunchy, and the food below is cooked. Serve immediately.

For stuffing recipes see pages 94–95, and for recipes using breadcrumbs in minced meat mixtures see pages 96–98.

# CRUNCHY SESAME AND POPCORN CHICKEN WITH HONEY AND TAMARI DIPPING SAUCE

**Using sesame seeds to create a crunchy coating, made lighter with crushed popcorn, provides a tasty and delicious alternative to breadcrumbs. Serve this dish at parties or as a sharing starter. As a variation, replace the chicken breasts with 3–5, raw peeled king prawns per person.**

• SERVES 4

4 free-range skinless boneless chicken breasts, cut into finger-width strips

• FOR THE MARINADE AND DIPPING SAUCE

2 tbsp runny honey
2 tbsp tamari
2 garlic cloves, finely chopped
zest and juice of 2 limes
1 red bird's eye chilli, finely sliced across its width
1 tbsp toasted sesame oil

• FOR THE COATING

25 g gluten-free salted popcorn, whizzed to crumbs
100 g white sesame seeds
2 medium eggs, beaten
4 tbsp rice flour
salt and freshly ground black pepper
1–2 tbsp vegetable oil

• FOR THE GARNISH

2 spring onions, sliced on the diagonal
handful coriander leaves, roughly chopped

To make the marinade and dipping sauce, mix the honey, tamari, garlic, lime zest and juice and chilli together. Pour half the mixture into a small serving bowl for the dipping sauce. Cover and chill. Stir the sesame oil into the remaining sauce and mix with the chicken strips. Cover and leave to marinate in the fridge for 1 hour.

Preheat the oven to 200°C.

To make the coating, mix the popcorn crumbs with the sesame seeds and season with salt and pepper. Tip into a wide, shallow dish.

Pour the beaten egg into a second wide, shallow dish, and spread the rice flour, seasoned with salt and pepper, over the bottom of a third shallow dish.

To coat the chicken strips, first dust each piece in rice flour, dip into the beaten egg, then evenly coat in the sesame seed mixture.

Arrange the coated chicken on the bottom of a roasting tin. Drizzle with vegetable oil, and bake for 15–20 minutes until the coating is golden and crisp, and the chicken is cooked through.

To serve, arrange the chicken on a serving plate, around the dipping sauce and sprinkle over the spring onion and coriander as a garnish. Serve immediately.

# CRUMBED HADDOCK GOUJONS

- SERVES 4

vegetable oil for deep-frying
2 tbsp rice flour seasoned with salt and pepper
225 g gluten-free white bread, whizzed into fine breadcrumbs
2 eggs, beaten
450 g skinned haddock fillet, sliced across into finger-sized strips
lemon wedges, to serve

- FOR THE GARLIC MAYONNAISE

290 ml good-quality mayonnaise
2 garlic cloves, crushed
salt and freshly ground black pepper

- VARIATION: RAVIGOTE SAUCE, SERVES 4

2 tsp red wine vinegar
2 tsp Dijon mustard
3 tbsp extra virgin olive oil
2 tsp salted capers, rinsed and roughly chopped
2 tbsp finely chopped flat leaf parsley
1 tbsp chopped tarragon
1 medium red onion, finely diced
salt and freshly ground black pepper

In a medium bowl, mix the vinegar, mustard, salt and pepper together. Slowly pour in the oil, whisking continuously until the sauce is thick and emulsified. Stir in the capers, parsley, tarragon and red onion and serve in a bowl with the haddock goujons.

**These make a great alternative to bought fish fingers. They are also very popular as a starter or as finger food with drinks. Serve lightly sprinkled with salt and lemon wedges or with garlic mayonnaise. For a more formal affair, try Sauce Ravigote.**

To make the garlic mayonnaise, stir the garlic into the mayonnaise, and lightly season with salt and pepper. Set aside.

Fill a heavy pan no more than one-third full of vegetable oil. Heat the oil over a low to medium heat until it reaches 180°C. Maintain the oil at this temperature over a low heat.

Place the rice flour and breadcrumbs on separate large plates, and pour the eggs into a wide, shallow dish. Roll the pieces of fish in the seasoned flour. This will help the egg to stick to the fish. Dip the floured fish into the beaten egg, then roll in the breadcrumbs until evenly coated. Gently shake the breaded fish above the dish to remove any loose crumbs.

Carefully slide a handful of crumbed fish into the hot oil, gently turning the goujons over in the oil so that they cook evenly. The goujons are cooked when they are crisp, golden brown and float to the surface.

Lift the goujons out of the oil with a slotted spoon onto a baking sheet covered with absorbent kitchen paper. Sprinkle with salt. Keep warm in a low oven with the door ajar so that the air can circulate around the fish to keep them crisp while you cook the rest.

Fry the remaining fish, by the handful, in the same way. To serve, pile the goujons high on a warm plate, squeeze over some lemon juice and serve immediately with the garlic mayonnaise and lemon wedges.

Serve these goujons with Ravigote Sauce (see left) as a tangy and colourful alternative to garlic mayonnaise.

*Tip*

**For variety, replace the haddock with strips of chicken breast, and season the breadcrumbs with paprika or a spice and herb mix of your choice.**

# GAZPACHO

**A refreshing, nutritious soup bursting with colour, flavour and goodness. The soup is thickened slightly with breadcrumbs to give it substance. Serve in shot glasses as a canapé with drinks, as a starter or as part of a picnic or barbecue on a hot summer's day.**

- SERVES 6

2 slices gluten-free white bread, whizzed to breadcrumbs
125 ml extra virgin oil
4 tbsp sherry vinegar
6 ripe tomatoes, deseeded and chopped
400 g tinned chopped tomatoes
1 red pepper, deseeded and diced
1 green pepper, deseeded and diced
1 medium onion, diced
3 garlic cloves, crushed
1 medium cucumber, peeled and diced
large pinch of sugar
250 ml cold water
salt and freshly ground black pepper

- FOR THE GARNISH

½ red pepper, deseeded and diced
½ green pepper, deseeded and diced
½ cucumber, diced
small handful of chives, finely sliced
2 tbsp extra virgin olive oil
pinch of salt
12 ice cubes
4 tbsp small croutons (page 47)

Soak the breadcrumbs in the oil and sherry vinegar for 15 minutes.

In a blender, whiz the fresh and tinned tomatoes, peppers, onion, garlic, cucumber, sugar and water to a thin purée. Add the bread, oil and vinegar mixture. Whiz until smooth.

Season with salt and pepper as needed. Chill for 1 hour.

To serve, ladle into bowls and garnish each serving with a handful of diced peppers and cucumber, chives, a drizzle of oil and 2 ice cubes per bowl. Scatter with the croutons. Serve immediately.

# SPICED LAMB & PISTACHIO KOFTA WITH HOMEMADE HOUMOUS

• SERVES 4

• FOR THE HOUMOUS

400 g tinned chickpeas, drained
juice of 2 lemons
2 garlic cloves, crushed
2 tbsp tahini or peanut butter
2 tbsp water
4 tbsp extra virgin olive oil
large pinch of salt and black pepper

• FOR THE KOFTAS – MAKES 18–20

800 g lamb mince
50 g pistachio nuts, roughly chopped
1 tbsp chopped mint
1 tbsp chopped flat-leaf parsley
1 tbsp chopped coriander
1 medium onion, finely diced
2 garlic cloves, finely chopped
3–4 tsp ras el hanout (see opposite)
1 tsp dried chilli flakes
zest of 1 lemon
2 tbsp light olive oil for frying
salt and freshly ground black pepper

• TO SERVE

4 gluten-free pitta breads
2 Little Gem lettuces, thinly sliced across
1 lemon, cut into wedges
Harissa (see opposite)

**These Lebanese kofta are flavoured with ras el hanout, a spice blend that tastes at its best when freshly made (see opposite). If using a shop-bought blend, check that it is gluten-free. For some additional spice, finish off with a drizzle of harissa (see opposite). The kofta, shaped into bite-sized oval balls and served on mini kebab sticks with houmous or tzatziki, make great party food too. Tahini is a beige-coloured paste made from roasted and ground sesame seeds. It is served as a dip and used to flavour houmous and other North African and Middle Eastern sauces such as baba ghanoush (page 59). If you do not have tahini to hand for the houmous, use peanut butter instead for a really gutsy flavour.**

Preheat the oven to 200°C.

First make the houmous. Place all the ingredients in a food processor and blend to a smooth purée. Spoon the houmous into a serving bowl, cover and chill until just before serving.

To make the kofta, in a large bowl, mix the lamb mince with the pistachio nuts, herbs, onion, garlic, ras el hanout, chilli flakes and lemon zest. Season well with salt and pepper. Fry off some of the mixture and taste to check the seasoning. Once the seasoning is correct, using wet hands roll the mixture into small oval balls, each the size of a small chicken's egg, and slide 2 on each of 4 skewers.

Heat the olive oil in a large frying pan over a medium heat. When hot, place the skewers side by side in the pan. Turn the skewers a little every minute for 5–10 minutes until the kofta are golden brown. Transfer the kofta to a baking sheet and bake in the oven for a further 5 minutes, or until cooked through.

Meanwhile toast the pitta breads and slice open.

Spread 1 tablespoon of houmous inside each of the 4 pitta pockets. Next, being careful with the hot skewers, slide 2 koftes inside each pocket.

Divide the shredded lettuce among the 4 plates, arrange the pitta pockets on top and serve immediately with a lemon wedge and harissa on the side.

## RAS EL HANOUT

**This exotic North African spice blend varies from shop to shop, its name meaning a blend of the best spices the shop has to offer. Ras el hanout is used to add a subtle spice flavour and rose fragrance to stews, rice, couscous and marinades for meat, poultry and fish, and is seen a great deal in Moroccan dishes. Although it is readily available in good supermarkets, preparing this spice blend yourself will give you the freshest flavour.**

- 1 cinnamon stick, broken into small pieces
- 2 tsp whole cloves
- ½ tsp freshly grated nutmeg
- 2 tsp coriander seeds
- 2 tsp cumin seeds
- 2 tsp fennel seeds
- 2 tsp black mustard seeds
- large pinch of Damascan rose petals (available in Middle Eastern food shops)

Toast the spices in a dry frying pan over a gentle heat for 2–3 minutes until the seeds start to brown and pop, and become aromatic. Stir continuously for a further minute, then remove from the heat and pour into a mortar.

Add the rose petals to the toasted spices and grind to a powder with the pestle.

Store in an airtight container for 1–2 weeks.

## HARISSA

**Harissa is a fiery Tunisian red chilli and garlic paste. It is used as a condiment or to add heat, flavour and colour to stews, dips, marinades, rice and couscous. Ready-made harissa is available in good supermarkets, but it tastes best freshly made and can be stored in an airtight jar in the fridge, covered in a little olive oil, for up to 1 month.**

MAKES 2 HEAPED TBSP

- 1 tsp caraway seeds
- 1 tsp cumin seeds
- 6 fresh long red chillies, deseeded and finely chopped
- 3 garlic cloves, finely chopped
- large pinch of salt
- 2 tsp smoked paprika
- 50 ml extra virgin olive oil

Toast the caraway and cumin seeds in a dry frying pan over a medium heat until the seeds begin to brown and pop. Remove from the heat and pour into a mortar and grind to a powder with the pestle.

Place the chillies and garlic on a chopping board, and sprinkle over the salt. Continue chopping with a large knife until the mixture becomes a rough purée.

Place the chilli and garlic purée in a bowl, and stir in the ground, toasted spices, paprika and olive oil to form the paste. Cover and chill for at least 1 hour before using to allow the flavours to develop. Use as needed.

## ZA'ATAR SPICE BLEND

**Middle Eastern za'atar, is used to flavour meat, fish and dips. Sumac is a crimson spice produced from a small red stone fruit, related to peaches and plums. Za'atar is best made fresh, but is also available in good supermarkets.**

- 1 tbsp each of sesame seeds, fresh oregano and thyme leaves
- 1 tsp sumac
- pinch of salt

Toast the sesame seeds, oregano and thyme leaves in a dry pan over a gentle heat for 2-3 minutes, until the sesame seeds are golden brown. Pour the mixture into a mortar and leave to cool for 5 minutes. Add the sumac and salt to the mortar and lightly grind the mixture to a coarse powder. Use as needed or store in an airtight container for up to 2 weeks.

# BAKED ZA'ATAR & LEMON CHICKEN WITH LEBANESE BROWN RICE, POMEGRANATE, CHICKPEA & COURGETTE SALAD & TZATZIKI

• SERVES 4–6

4 large skinless boneless chicken breasts

• FOR THE MARINADE

juice of 1 lemon
2 tbsp light olive oil
2 tsp ground cumin
2 tsp smoked paprika
2 garlic cloves, crushed

• FOR THE SALAD

500 g brown basmati rice
1 red onion, sliced thinly
400 g tin chickpeas, drained
50 g pistachio nuts, roasted until golden brown
300 g courgettes, coarsely grated
1 pomegranate, halved
2 tbsp za'atar (page 55), to garnish

• FOR THE LEMON AND CUMIN DRESSING

juice of 2 lemons
2 tsp ground cumin
4 tbsp extra virgin olive oil
salt and black pepper

• FOR THE TZATZIKI

4 heaped tbsp thick Greek yoghurt
2 garlic cloves, crushed
1 small cucumber, coarsely grated
2 tsp lemon juice
salt and freshly ground black pepper

**A vibrantly coloured and satisfying salad, rich in texture and flavour. Perfect for barbecues and buffets.**

First cook the brown rice for the salad (see page 11), then cool under cold running water. Set aside.

Mix the marinade ingredients together in an ovenproof dish. Coat the chicken breasts in the marinade, cover and chill for 1–2 hours.

Meanwhile, mix the lemon and cumin dressing ingredients together and stir in the red onion. Cover and leave to marinate for 1 hour.

To make the tzatziki, mix the yoghurt, garlic, cucumber and lemon juice together. Season with salt and pepper. Cover and chill.

Preheat the oven to 200°C.

To make the rice salad, pour the cooked and cooled brown rice into a large serving dish, and stir in the chickpeas, pistachio nuts and courgette.

Remove the seeds from the pomegranate over a bowl, to catch any juice. Discard any membrane, and stir the seeds and juice into the rice salad.

Bake the chicken together with its marinade in the oven for 25 minutes until cooked through. Leave to cool in the hot marinade.

To finish the rice salad, stir in the marinated onion with its lemon and cumin dressing and half the cooked and cooled marinade. Taste and season with salt and pepper as needed and spoon into a serving dish. Sprinkle with 1 tablespoon of the za'atar.

To serve, thickly slice the chicken and arrange on top of the rice salad, then sprinkle with the remaining za'atar. Serve with tzatziki and the remaining cooled marinade from the chicken.

# CROQUE MONSIEUR

- MAKES 2 ROLLS OR SANDWICHES

100 g butter, at room temperature,
8 slices gluten-free white bread, crusts removed

- FOR THE CHEESE SAUCE

1 tbsp cornflour
200 ml milk
60 g Gruyère, grated
¼ tsp freshly grated nutmeg
pinch of salt and freshly ground black pepper

- FOR THE FILLING

1 tbsp Dijon mustard
4 slices good quality lean ham
60 g Gruyère, grated

**The French, rather more sophisticated version of a toasted cheese and ham sandwich, to enjoy at any time of the day, simply as it is or with a crisp and lightly dressed green salad.**

Preheat the grill to medium-high, and line a large baking sheet with foil.

Melt the butter in a pan, then remove from the heat. Brush one side of each slice of bread liberally with melted butter, and arrange side by side on the baking sheet, buttered side up.

Grill the buttered side of the bread until golden and crisp, then set aside.

To make the cheese sauce, stir the cornflour into the remaining butter to make a smooth paste, then stir over the heat for 1 minute. Remove the pan from the heat and gradually whisk in the milk. Bring the sauce to a gentle simmer over a low heat, stirring continuously until the sauce is smooth and thick. Continue to simmer for a further minute. Remove from the heat and stir in the Gruyère cheese until it is fully melted. Stir in the grated nutmeg, salt and 2 or 3 grinds of black pepper.

Generously spread the untoasted sides of 4 slices of the bread with the mustard and cover each one with a slice of ham, followed by a good sprinkling of the cheese.

Place the remaining slices of bread on top, toasted side up. Thickly spread the cheese sauce on top.

Place the 4 assembled croque monsieurs in the centre of the oven, well away from the grill, and slowly grill for 5–7 minutes until the cheese sauce is brown and bubbling, and the cheese filling has melted. Serve immediately.

# SPICED PITTA CHIPS

**These crunchy and richly spiced pitta chips make the perfect dipping partner for baba ghanoush, tzatziki and houmous – and they will go quickly!**

• SERVES 4

2 tbsp olive oil
2 garlic cloves, crushed
2 tsp ground cumin
2 tsp ground coriander
½ tsp cayenne pepper
large pinch of salt and freshly ground black pepper
4 white, brown or seeded gluten-free pitta breads, each cut diagonally across into 6 triangles

Preheat the oven to 200°C.

Combine the oil, garlic, spices and cayenne pepper in a large bowl.

Brush both sides of each pitta triangle with the spiced oil, and arrange in one layer over the bottom of a large baking sheet. Drizzle any remaining spiced oil over the pitta bread.

Bake in the oven for 5–7 minutes, then turn each pitta chip over once. Bake for a further 5–7 minutes until crisp and golden.

Serve warm, fresh from the oven, with dips.

## BEE'S SMASHED AVOCADO & GREEN PEA DIP

**My sister-in-law serves this bright-green nutritious dip with lamb and prawns straight off the barbecue.**

SERVES 4

- 2 ripe avocadoes, stoned, skinned and diced
- 200 g fresh or frozen pea
- 2 garlic cloves, crushed
- 3 spring onions, thinly sliced
- juice of ½ lemon
- 1 tbsp extra virgin olive oil
- large pinch of salt and freshly ground black pepper
- 1 tbsp chopped mint

Place the avocado into a bowl. Bring the peas to the boil, then drain and cool in a sieve under cold, running water. Add the peas, crushed garlic, spring onion, lemon juice, olive oil to the avocado. Season with salt and pepper.

Using a potato masher, crush the avocado and peas to a rough purée. Stir in the mint. Taste and season as needed. Serve immediately.

## BABA GHANOUSH

**Serve this smooth and delicate Middle Eastern dip with toasted pitta or vegetable crudités.**

SERVES 4–6

- 2 large aubergines
- 2 garlic cloves, crushed
- 2 tbsp tahini paste
- juice of 1 lemon
- 1 tbsp extra virgin olive oil
- salt and freshly ground black pepper

Preheat the oven to 220°C.

Place the aubergines on a baking sheet, and roast for 20 minutes, or until the aubergine flesh is soft to the centre. Remove from the oven and leave to cool.

Halve the aubergines, and scoop out the flesh with a spoon into a food processor. Add the garlic, tahini, lemon juice, olive oil and season with salt and pepper. Process until smooth.

Spoon into a serving bowl, drizzle with olive oil and serve.

# SANDWICHES

**It is so easy to make the same old sandwich for lunch every day. To make lunch or a light snack more interesting, try one of these fillings, or arrange on 2 slices of buttered bread to make an open sandwich.**

## CHARGRILLED CHICKEN, WATERCRESS, ORANGE AND MINT

**This summery filling tastes best in seeded or brown rolls and bread. The ingredients also look beautiful arranged on an open sandwich. Marinate your chicken for at least 1 hour before grilling or barbecuing, to enhance the flavour.**

MAKES 2 ROLLS OR SANDWICHES

- 2 gluten-free seeded rolls, sliced in half or 4 slices of gluten-free seeded or brown bread, buttered

FOR THE MARINADE

- 2 tbsp extra virgin olive oil
- zest and juice of 1 orange
- 1 large garlic clove, crushed
- 2 grinds of black pepper
- 1 large skinless boneless chicken breast, sliced through lengthways

FOR THE SALAD GARNISH

- handful watercress
- 1 medium orange, peeled and sliced into thin rounds
- 1 spring onion, finely sliced
- 4 mint leaves, finely chopped
- 1 tbsp extra virgin olive oil
- pinch of salt and 2 grinds of black pepper

Blend the marinade ingredients together in a bowl large enough to hold a chicken breast. Place the chicken breast in the bowl, and coat with the marinade. Cover and leave to marinate in the fridge for at least 30 minutes.

Preheat the grill or barbecue.

Meanwhile, toss the watercress, orange, spring onion and mint with the olive oil in a large bowl. Season with salt and pepper and toss again. Set aside.

Remove the chicken from the fridge and lift out of the marinade. Place on a baking sheet, and grill for 3 minutes on each side, or until lightly charred and cooked through, brushing with the marinade at least once on each side. Thickly slice the chicken and arrange on the base of the 2 split rolls or bread slices.

Place a small handful of the salad on top of the chicken, gently press the top half of each roll or bread slices in place and serve immediately.

## TUNA NIÇOISE

**A taste of Provence in a sandwich. This filling also makes a very attractive open sandwich topping, thanks to the many colourful ingredients.**

MAKES 2 SANDWICHES

- 1 x 160g tin tuna in sunflower or olive oil, drained and broken up into small chunks
- 4 anchovy fillets, roughly chopped
- 2 tsp capers, rinsed and dried, roughly chopped
- 1 heaped tbsp good-quality mayonnaise
- 3 grinds black pepper
- 2 gluten-free rolls or 4 slices of gluten-free white, brown or seeded bread
- butter for spreading
- 1 tbsp pitted and roughly chopped kalamata olives
- 2 ripe tomatoes, thinly sliced
- 1 medium hard-boiled egg, sliced
- ½ red onion, thinly sliced
- handful of baby salad leaves

In a bowl, mix the tuna, anchovies, capers, mayonnaise and black pepper together.

Butter the 2 rolls or 4 slices of bread.

Divide the tuna mixture evenly among the rolls or bread.

Sprinkle over the olives, then arrange the tomato slices, sliced egg and a sprinkling of red onion in layers. Lastly, top the filling with baby salad leaves, and cover with the roll tops or slices of bread.

Slice the sandwiches on the diagonal and enjoy!

## NEW YORK DELI

**This top seller originating from New York is quick to make and a welcome change from ham and cheese. Great in seeded and brown bread or rolls.**

MAKES 2 ROLLS OR SANDWICHES

- 1 tbsp mayonnaise
- 2 tsp Dijon mustard
- 3 grinds black pepper
- 4 slices gluten-free seeded bread, buttered
- 8 slices deli-style pastrami
- 4 square slices Gruyère cheese
- 1 small red onion, thinly sliced
- 2 large dill pickles, thinly sliced lengthways
- 1 Little Gem lettuce, broken into leaves, washed and dried

In a bowl, mix the mayonnaise, mustard and black pepper together. Spread on all 4 bread slices.

Arrange 2 slices of pastrami and 1 slice of Gruyère cheese slice on 1 bread slice, then prepare a second slice in the same way.

Arrange red onion rings, dill pickle slices and 3 Little Gem leaves on top. Gently press the remaining slices of bread in place to make sandwiches.

Cut the sandwiches in half and serve immediately.

# WARM BACON, CHORIZO, EGG & POTATO SALAD WITH WARM MUSTARD DRESSING

• SERVES 4–6

1 kg waxy salad potatoes such as Charlotte or Vivaldi
4 eggs
1 tbsp extra virgin olive oil
250 g smoked bacon lardons
100 g gluten-free chorizo, skin removed, thinly sliced
1 large onion, thinly sliced
250 g fine green beans, topped and tailed
2 tbsp coarsely chopped chives

• FOR THE DRESSING

2 tbsp red wine vinegar
2 tsp Dijon mustard
6 tbsp extra virgin olive oil
salt and freshly ground black pepper

**This warm salad makes the most of the perfect flavour and textural combination of bacon, egg, new potatoes and al dente green beans, spiced with chorizo. Serve for brunch, lunch or a quick and satisfying supper.**

Boil the potatoes until just tender, and then keep warm in the oven.

Put the eggs in a small saucepan, cover with water and bring to the boil. Continue boiling for 3½ minutes, so they are just set in the middle. Remove from the heat, drain and peel the ends under cool, running water. Set aside while you prepare the remaining ingredients.

In a medium frying pan, heat the olive oil and fry the bacon lardons and chorizo until golden brown and crisp. Lift out of the fat with a slotted spoon, and keep warm in the oven with the potatoes.

Using the same pan, fry the sliced onion in the bacon fat until soft, and add to the bacon and chorizo in the oven.

Steam the green beans until al dente.

To make the dressing, mix the red wine vinegar and Dijon mustard, together thoroughly in a small bowl. Season with a pinch of salt and a few grinds of pepper. Mix in the olive oil. Taste and adjust the seasoning if necessary.

Thickly slice the potatoes into a large bowl. Add the dressing, along with the onions, bacon, chorizo and green beans. Gently mix the ingredients together and spoon onto warm plates. Cut the eggs in half and arrange 2 halves on each salad. Sprinkle with chives and serve immediately while the salad is warm.

# HOT SMOKED SALMON, DILL PICKLE & POTATO SALAD WITH SOURED CREAM DRESSING

- SERVES 4

1 kg waxy potatoes such as Charlotte or Vivaldi
4 shallots, finely diced
1 tbsp pickling liquor from the dill pickles
200 g dill pickles, sliced thinly on the diagonal
300 ml soured cream
1 bunch of dill, coarsely chopped
large pinch of salt and 4 grinds of black pepper
400 g hot-smoked salmon or trout, broken into large flakes

**This salad works really well with flaked smoked salmon or trout, or sliced smoked chicken breast too. Serve as part of a buffet or on individual plates with a lightly dressed green salad.**

Boil the potaoes in their skins until just tender in the centre, then cool.

Mix the shallots with the pickling liquor and leave to marinate for 15 minutes to soften.

Meanwhile, peel the boiled potatoes, then thickly slice and place in a large bowl. Add the sliced pickles and toss through gently.

Mix the soured cream with the marinated shallots and half the dill, then season with a large pinch of salt and the pepper. Mix the dressing into the potatoes.

In a large salad bowl or on individual plates, layer the potato mixture with flakes of hot smoked salmon, then sprinkle with the remaining dill to garnish.

# HAM, CHEESE & JALAPEÑO QUESADILLAS SERVED WITH SWEETCORN & AVOCADO SALSA & SOUR CREAM

**Warming, easy to prepare and great served with guacamole.**

First, make the sweetcorn and avocado salsa by mixing all the salsa ingredients together in a medium bowl. Season with salt and pepper. Cover and set aside.

To make the quesadillas, preheat the oven to 80°C. Place the 4 tortillas on a large chopping board, and cover each with a slice of ham, then spread the grated cheese over one half of each tortilla, followed by a quarter of the jalapeño peppers on each. Fold each tortilla in half to form 4 semicircular quesadillas.

Heat a dry frying pan or ridged grill pan over a medium heat.

Brush both sides of each quesadilla with the vegetable oil. Place two in the heated pan and cook for a minute. Using a fish slice, carefully flip over and cook for further minute on the second side or until the tortilla is crisp and the cheese inside has melted. Transfer to the oven for 2 minutes, to ensure the cheese is melted completely. Repeat with the remaining 2 quesadillas.

Using the fish slice, transfer each quesadilla to a chopping board and cut in half. Arrange the quesadillas on 4 plates with a spoonful of sweetcorn salsa.

Serve immediately with soured cream.

- SERVES 4

- FOR THE QUESADILLAS

4 gluten-free tortilla
4 slices good-quality lean ham
2 tbsp pickled jalapeño chillies, drained
100 g mature Cheddar cheese, coarsely grated
vegetable oil for brushing the quesadillas

- FOR THE SWEETCORN SALSA

190 g tinned sweetcorn
1 medium avocado, peeled, stoned and diced into 1-cm cubes
200 g ripe cherry tomatoes, quartered
3 spring onions, finely sliced
½–1 medium-red chilli, deseeded and finely chopped.
2 garlic cloves, finely chopped
zest and juice of 1 lime
large pinch of salt and freshly ground black pepper
handful coriander leaves, roughly chopped
300 ml soured cream, to serve

# KING PRAWNS & WILD RICE, SAUTÉED WITH GARLIC, BLACK PEPPER & LIME

**This recipe originates from a memorable lunch in a very simple café in Hong Kong. The prawns were simply sautéed with freshly ground black pepper and salt, and served in the wok with wedges of lime, and we all tucked into what was the most delicious meal I have ever tasted. The black rice adds a dramatic contrast to the pink prawns and absorbs their delicious juices.**

• SERVES 4
100 g wild rice
2 tbsp vegetable oil
20 raw king or tiger prawns
6 garlic cloves, finely chopped
1 medium fresh red chilli, deseeded and finely chopped
3 spring onions, thinly sliced on the diagonal
handful of coriander leaves, roughly chopped
zest and juice of 1 lime
1 tsp caster sugar
salt and freshly ground black pepper

• FOR THE GARNISH
1 lime, cut into 4 wedges
4 coriander sprigs

First, cook the wild rice (page 11).

In a wok or large frying pan, heat the vegetable oil until it is just beginning to smoke.

Add half the prawns to the pan, season with a pinch of salt and 3 grinds of pepper, sauté for about 3 minutes until the prawns are fully pink and cooked through. Transfer to a plate.

Heat another tablespoon of oil in the pan, if needed, and fry the remaining prawns in the same way, once again seasoning with salt and pepper.

Return all the prawns to the pan, stir in the cooked wild rice, garlic, chilli, spring onions and chopped coriander. Sir-fry for 30 seconds.

Stir in the lime zest and juice and the sugar, then taste a little of the rice to check that the vibrant flavours are coming through. Add another pinch of salt and sugar if needed.

Divide the prawns and rice among 4 plates, spoon on any sauce collected in the pan and serve immediately, each topped with a sprig of coriander and a wedge of lime.

# SAVOURY BRETON BUCKWHEAT CRÊPES

• SERVES 4 – MAKES 8

110 g buckwheat flour, or 55 g each of buckwheat flour and rice flour
½ tsp fine salt
290 ml milk, dairy-free milk or water
2 eggs, beaten
2 tbsp vegetable oil

**Buckwheat flour is traditionally used in pancakes, blinis and galettes, particularly in Brittany, Eastern Europe and Russia. It gives pancakes a characteristic light brown colour and nutty flavour. Use these crêpes to make Breton galettes filled with ham, eggs and Gruyère cheese for a savoury light meal.**

To make the crêpe batter, sift the buckwheat flour and salt into a large bowl, and make a well in the centre.

Mix the milk into the beaten eggs until well combined, and pour half of this mixture into the flour well.

With a wooden spoon, stir the egg and milk mixture in small circles to gradually draw the flour into the liquid. As the egg mixture thickens, gradually pour the remaining liquid into the well and continue to stir until all the flour is incorporated and a smooth batter is achieved. Do not worry if you have a few lumps; just pass the batter through a sieve to remove them.

Stir in 1 tablespoon of the oil, then cover with cling film and chill for 30 minutes.

When you are ready to cook the crêpes, remove the batter from the fridge and stir well. Heat the remaining oil in a large frying pan, gently swirling the pan to oil the base evenly. Pour out any excess oil into a bowl. Return the pan to the heat. When the remaining oil starts to smoke, pour in sufficient batter that, when swirled around, it covers the base of the pan. Tip any excess batter back into the bowl.

After 30 seconds or so, when bubbles start to appear on the surface of the crêpe and the edge begins to brown, use a palette knife to loosen the pancake and flip it over and cook the other side for a further 30 seconds.

Lift the crêpe out of the pan onto a plate. Cover with foil and repeat the process until you have used all the batter and have made at least 8 crêpes.

*Tip*

**For a milder flavour, replace half the buckwheat flour with fine rice flour.**

# BRETON HAM, EGG & CHEESE GALETTES (CRÊPE COMPLÈTE)

**Crêpe complète makes a very good light lunch or evening meal served with a lightly dressed green salad.**

- SERVES 4

4 freshly cooked Savoury Breton Buckwheat Crêpes (see opposite)
4 slices good-quality ham
4 eggs
100 g Gruyère cheese, grated

To assemble each crêpe, place a frying pan over a medium heat. Slice a freshly made crêpe into the pan, and place a slice of ham in the centre. Crack an egg onto the centre of the ham, and sprinkle a quarter of the cheese over the top.

Allow the egg to cook for 30 seconds, then fold the edges of the crêpe onto the egg whites, to form a square with the yolk still visible in the centre. The melting cheese will hold the edges of the folded crêpe in place.

Reduce the heat to low and continue cooking the crêpe until the egg whites are just set and the yolk is still runny.

Lift out of the pan and onto a warmed plate. Serve immediately.

# SAVOURY BUCKWHEAT CRÊPES FILLED WITH SPINACH & RICOTTA IN ITALIAN TOMATO SAUCE

**A classic Italian dish, perfect for informal lunches and suppers. This recipe makes 6 large stuffed crêpes, and my family are agreed that, although delicious, one crêpe each is perfect.**

- MAKES 8

1 quantity of Savoury Breton Buckwheat Crêpe batter (page 68)

- FOR THE FILLING

500 g washed fresh spinach
50 g Parmesan, finely grated
500 g ricotta cheese
large pinch of grated nutmeg
pinch of salt and freshly ground black pepper

- FOR THE TOPPING

2 x 125 g balls of buffalo mozzarella, thinly sliced
50 g Parmesan, finely grated

1 quantity of Italian Tomato Sauce (page 99)

To make the filling, put the spinach in a large pan with a close-fitting lid over a low heat. Gently cook for 5 minutes, stirring occasionally, until the spinach has reduced in volume by two-thirds. Tip the spinach into a colander, and press firmly against the sides of the colander with the back of a wooden spoon to remove excess liquid. Leave to cool.

When completely cooled, roughly chop the spinach and mix in a large bowl with the Parmesan and ricotta. Season well with the nutmeg, salt and pepper.

Preheat the oven to 200°C.

Spread the tomato sauce evenly over the bottom of a large, rectangular ovenproof dish.

To assemble the crêpes, place 2 crêpes at a time on a chopping board. Place 2 tablespoons of ricotta and spinach mixture in a line across the center of each crêpe. Like a spring roll, fold the bottom half of each crêpe over the filling. Fold in the edges to seal in the filling, then roll up to form a sealed cylinder.

Arrange the filled crêpes in a line over the tomato sauce and cover with mozzarella slices. Sprinkle with the Parmesan and season with the pepper.

Bake the crêpes in the oven for 30–40 minutes until the cheese is golden and bubbling. Remove from the oven and leave to cool for 5 minutes before serving.

# ROSY RAW FENNEL, BEETROOT & CARROT SALAD WITH BUCKWHEAT & TOASTED ALMONDS

- SERVES 4

100 g roasted buckwheat groats
1 fennel bulb, cut lengthways, then thinly sliced across
1 medium beetroot, washed, peeled and thinly sliced across into discs
1 large carrot, thinly sliced on the diagonal
1 Granny Smith apple, peeled, cored, quartered and thinly sliced across
1 medium red onion, thinly sliced
30 g toasted flaked almonds
2 tbsp roughly chopped flat-leaf parsley
salt and freshly ground black pepper

- FOR THE DRESSING

2 heaped tsp wholegrain mustard
1 tbsp cider vinegar
3 tbsp extra virgin oil
large pinch of salt and 3 grinds of freshly ground black pepper

**This rosy pink, zingy salad is a beautiful dish for a buffet. I recommend you use a mandolin to slice the vegetables very thinly. Serve with hot or cold chicken, salmon, ham, sausage or smoked fish such as mackerel.**

Cook the roasted buckwheat groats (page 11) and cool in a seive under cold, running water.

To make the dressing, mix the mustard and cider vinegar with a large pinch of salt and 3 grinds of pepper, then whisk in the olive oil.

Put the fennel, beetroot, carrot, apple and red onion in a salad bowl, toss through the dressing and leave to stand for 5 minutes.

Mix in the cooked buckwheat groats, almond flakes and parsley. Season to taste with salt and pepper, and serve immediately or cover and chill for up to 24 hours before eating.

# WARM PUY LENTIL, GOAT'S CHEESE, SMOKED BACON & BABY SPINACH SALAD

- SERVES 4

2 tbsp light olive oil
160 g smoked bacon lardons or smoked streaky bacon, thinly sliced
4 spring onions, thinly sliced
2 garlic cloves, finely chopped
1 tbsp fresh thyme leaves
1 tbsp balsamic vinegar
800 g tinned Puy lentils, washed under cold, running water and drained
2 large handfuls of baby spinach leaves, washed
150 g fresh goat's cheese, roughly chopped

**This traditional French salad is delicious, nutritious, attractive and, most importantly, very quick to prepare. Enjoy the salad as it is or serve with new potatoes and a crisp green salad.**

Heat the olive oil in a large frying pan over a medium heat, and fry the lardons or sliced bacon until golden and crisp. Stir in the spring onions, garlic and thyme and fry for a further 30 seconds until aromatic. Stir in the balsamic vinegar and drained Puy lentils, and stir for 5–10 minutes until warmed through. Stir in the spinach leaves and cook for a further minute, or until the leaves have just wilted.

Spoon the lentil salad onto a warm serving dish, sprinkle with the goat's cheese and serve immediately.

# QUINOA, ROASTED TOMATOES, BLACK OLIVE & HERB SALAD

**Quinoa's light and fluffy texture goes beautifully with the flavours of Provence. Enjoy this salad with meat, poultry or fish, as part of an informal meal or buffet.**

- SERVES 4

5 thyme sprigs
12 ripe vine cherry tomatoes, halved
3 garlic cloves, thinly sliced lengthways
2 tbsp extra virgin olive oil
120 g quinoa, rinsed under cold, running water
1 tbsp chopped flat-leaf parsley
1 large handful of basil leaves, shredded
100 g black provençal or kalamata olives
salt and freshly ground black pepper

Preheat the oven to 170°C.

Scatter the thyme sprigs in the bottom of a roasting tray, followed by the cherry tomatoes, cut side up. Next, scatter with the garlic, drizzle over the olive oil, sprinkle over a large pinch of salt and season with pepper.

Roast the tomatoes in the oven for 45 minutes, or until they have dried to half their size and are slightly browned on top. Remove from the oven and leave to cool in the tin, reserving any cooking juices.

Meanwhile, place the quinoa in a medium pan and cover with 360 ml of cold salted water. Cook as per the instructions on page 11, then spoon into the serving dish to cool.

Once the quinoa is cool, add the cooled roasted tomatoes, parsley, basil and olives to the bowl.

To make the dressing, first mix the sherry vinegar with a pinch of salt and freshly ground black pepper into the reserved cooking juices from the tomatoes, then whisk in 1 tablespoon of olive oil.

Tip the dressing into the quinoa mixture, gently mixing all the ingredients together.

Either serve the salad at room temperature, soon after it is made, or cover, chill and eat within 24 hours.

• FOR THE DRESSING
1 tbsp sherry vinegar
1 tbsp extra virgin oil
salt and freshly ground black pepper

# ROASTED TOMATO, AUBERGINE, LENTIL & HARISSA SOUP WITH MINTED YOGHURT

**A substantial soup bursting with goodness and Mediterranean flavours. Serve with a spoonful of cool, creamy Greek yoghurt mixed with mint and lime juice.**

Preheat the oven to 170°C. Spread the halved tomatoes, cut side up, and the aubergine slices over the bottom of a large roasting tray. Drizzle with 3 tablespoons of the olive oil and season with salt and pepper. Bake for 1 hour, or until the tomatoes have reduced by a third in size and are beginning to brown. The aubergine should be soft and golden brown.

Meanwhile, in a large saucepan gently fry the onion in the remaining oil until soft and slightly browned. Add the garlic, spices and harissa, and fry for a further 30 seconds.

Pour the stock into the pan, followed by the roasted tomatoes and aubergines, any cooking juices and the apricots. Bring to the boil and simmer for 10 minutes.

Mix the Greek yoghurt with half the chopped mint and lime juice.

Blend the soup until smooth, then add the drained lentils. Bring the soup back to simmering point.

Ladle into bowls and garnish with a swirl of the minted yoghurt and some extra chopped mint.

• SERVES 4–6
800 g ripe vine tomatoes, halved
2 medium aubergines, cut lengthways into 1-cm thick slices
4 tbsp extra virgin olive oil
2 onions, thinly sliced
4 garlic cloves, finely chopped
1 tsp ground cumin
1 tsp ground coriander
1 tsp smoked paprika
1½ tsp harissa (page 55)
500 ml chicken or vegetable stock
8 dried apricots
400 g tinned lentils, drained
salt and freshly ground black pepper

• TO SERVE
250 ml thick Greek yoghurt
2 tbsp chopped mint, plus extra to garnish
1 tsp lime juice

# GREEN VEGETABLE MINESTRONE WITH PARSLEY, ALMOND & LEMON GREMOLATA

• SERVES 6

2 tbsp light olive oil
4 spring onions, finely sliced
2 garlic cloves, finely chopped
200 ml white wine
1.3 litres rich chicken stock
2 small courgettes, finely diced
100 g Savoy cabbage leaves, thinly sliced
200 g frozen peas
large handful baby spinach leaves, washed
100 g gluten-free fusilli pasta, cooked and roughly chopped
1 tbsp finely chopped flat-leaf parsley
1 tbsp finely shredded basil
50 g Parmesan, finely grated
salt and freshly ground black pepper

• FOR THE GREMOLATA

50 g blanched almonds
zest of 1 lemon
1 tbsp finely chopped flat-leaf parsley

**The secret to making this aromatic soup filled with fresh green vegetables is to prepare all the ingredients in advance, then cook them just before eating.**

To make the gremolata, first toast the almonds in a dry frying pan until golden brown, then chop finely. Mix the almonds with the lemon zest and parsley in a bowl. Set aside.

Gently heat the olive oil in a large pan, and fry the spring onions and garlic for 30 seconds. Increase the heat, add the wine and simmer for 1 minute. Pour in the stock and bring to a gentle boil.

Add the courgettes, cabbage and peas, and simmer for 2 minutes. Add the spinach, cooked pasta, chopped herbs and Parmesan, then simmer for a further minute.

Ladle the soup into four warm bowls, sprinkle with the gremolata and serve immediately.

# THAI PORK, MANGO, CORIANDER & RICE NOODLE SALAD

• SERVES 4–6

600 g whole pork fillet
handful of coriander leaves roughly chopped, to garnish

• FOR THE CORIANDER MARINADE

large handful of coriander, roughly chopped
2 garlic cloves, finely chopped
zest of 1 lime
1 tsp caster sugar
1 tbsp fish sauce
1 tbsp tamari
freshly ground black pepper

• FOR THE SALAD

1 large firm mango
3 spring onions, finely sliced
1 tbsp roughly chopped coriander
1 tbsp roughly chopped mint
½ red onion, thinly sliced
1 long fresh red chilli, deseeded and finely sliced
½ cucumber
large handful of beansprouts
500 g fine fresh rice noodles

• FOR THE DRESSING

zest and juice of 2 limes
2 tbsp fish sauce
2 tsp soft brown sugar

**This fat-free, zingy salad is full of mouth-watering exciting flavours and chilli spice. Serve for a light meal, a starter or as part of a buffet. This recipe makes generous quantities because everyone will want more.**

First, mix the marinade ingredients together in a bowl, and pour over the pork fillet placed in an ovenproof dish. Turn the fillets over in the marinade until thoroughly coated, cover and chill for at least 30 minutes. Meanwhile, preheat the oven to 200°C.

Bake the marinated pork fillet for 30 minutes, or until firm when pressed but with a hint of rosiness remaining in the centre of the fillet. Leave to cool in the marinade.

Prepare the salad ingredients. Peel and stone the mango, then slice into matchsticks. Halve the cucumber lengthways, remove the seeds with a spoon and slice thinly into half-moons on the diagonal. Refresh the noodles in boiling water for 1 minute, then drain and cool under cold, running water. Finally, mix together all the ingredients.

Mix the dressing ingredients together.

Slice the pork thinly on the diagonal, and mix with the cooked marinade juices, reserving some of the marinade.

Heap the salad onto 4 plates, then arrange 3–5 pork slices on top. Spoon over a little of the reserved marinade and garnish with coriander leaves.

*Tip*

**For variation, replace the pork with 4 chicken breasts or 4 sea bass fillets, marinated and baked in the oven until cooked through.**

# CHIANG MAI NOODLE SOUP

**This bright yellow, richly flavoured noodle soup is a speciality of the Thai city Chiang Mai. It is simple to make and absolutely delicious, so don't be put off by the long ingredients list.**

First, make the curry paste. Toast the cumin and coriander seeds in a dry frying pan until aromatic, then place all the paste ingredients in a food processor or use a pestle and mortar. Chop or grind until the ingredients come together into a smooth paste.

To make the soup, in a large pan, bring the coconut milk and chicken stock to a simmer. Stir in 1–2 tablespoons of the curry paste (depending on your spice preference). Stir in the turmeric and brown sugar, and simmer for 2 minutes.

Add the chicken and poach gently for 10 minutes, or until the chicken is cooked through.

Add the fish sauce and tamari. Simmer gently for 7–10 minutes. Remove from the heat and stir in the lime juice. Taste and season with more fish sauce and tamari as needed.

Blanch the rice noodles in boiling water, then drain and divide among 4 warm bowls. Divide the chicken evenly among each serving, then ladle over the coconut soup.

To garnish, mix together the spring and red onions, coriander and beansprouts, then pile on top of the noodles and soup. Serve immediately.

• SERVES 4–6

• FOR THE CURRY PASTE

2 tsp cumin seeds
2 tsp coriander seeds
4 grinds of ground black pepper
pinch salt
2 tsp red chilli flakes
2 cm-thick slice of ginger, peeled and roughly chopped
1 stalk lemon grass, tough outer leaves removed, finely sliced
zest of 1 lime
1 tbsp chopped coriander stems
½ red onion, finely diced
2 garlic cloves, chopped
2 tsp shrimp paste
2 fresh red bird's-eye chillies, deseeded and roughly chopped

• FOR THE SOUP

400 ml coconut milk
400 ml rich chicken stock
1 tsp ground turmeric
1 tsp light brown soft sugar
8 skinless chicken thigh fillets, trimmed of fat and thinly sliced
1 tbsp fish sauce
1 tbsp tamari
juice of 1 lime
500 g fresh rice noodles

• FOR THE GARNISH

3 spring onions, finely sliced
1 red onion, finely diced
large handful, coriander leaves
large handful, beansprouts

# CARROT, ORANGE & HAZELNUT SOUP WITH ORANGE GREMOLATA

- SERVES 8

100 g hazelnuts
1 tbsp hazelnut oil, plus extra to serve
1 kg carrots, chopped
2 onions, cut into large dice
4 garlic cloves, finely chopped
finely grated zest and juice of 1 orange
1 litre chicken or vegetable stock
2 bay leaves
4 thyme sprigs
6 flat-leaf parsley stalks
salt and freshly ground black pepper

- FOR THE GREMOLATA

finely grated zest of 1 orange
1 tbsp roughly chopped flat-leaf parsley

**This soup is a vibrant orange, with a delicate orange and nutty scent. Perfect for lunch or as a starter either hot or chilled. For a simpler soup, replace the gremolata with croutons (page 47).**

First, toast the hazelnuts in a dry frying pan until golden brown, then chop roughly. Set aside.

Gently heat the hazelnut oil in a medium pan and add the carrots. Season with salt and pepper, cover and leave to soften without colouring. This could take 20–30 minutes.

Add the garlic and orange zest, and gently fry for 30 seconds.

Pour in the orange juice and stock, add the bay leaves, thyme, parsley stalks and half the hazelnuts, then bring to a simmer. Simmer for 20 minutes, or until the carrot is very soft.

Remove the parsley stalks, thyme sprigs and bay leaves from the pan with a slotted spoon and blend or process the soup until smooth.

Mix the remaining hazelnuts and the rest of the gremolata ingredients together.

Ladle the soup into warm bowls, sprinkle the gremolata on top and lightly drizzle with the extra hazelnut oil. Serve the soup immediately.

# CLASSIC SAUSAGE ROLLS

**Making the sausagemeat yourself enables you to add different flavouring ingredients. Cut into large sausage rolls for warming light meals or into mini rolls for parties.**

- MAKES 4 LARGE OR 8 SMALL

- FOR THE SAUSAGEMEAT

450 g pork mince
½ onion, finely diced
2 tbsp gluten-free white breadcrumbs
1 tbsp finely chopped thyme, parsley and sage leaves
1 garlic clove, finely chopped
large pinch of fine salt and 4 grinds of freshly ground black pepper

- FOR THE PASTRY

1 x 400g block gluten-free puff pastry, defrosted to room temperature
1 egg, beaten

Preheat the oven to 200°C.

In a large bowl, mix all the sausagemeat ingredients together with your hands. Fry a small flattened ball of the sausagemeat in a little oil until cooked through and taste to check the seasoning. Season the sausage meat again if needed.

Roll out the puff pastry into a large rectangle 3 mm thick, then cut into 2 long rectangles.

Roll the sausage meat into a sausage the length of the pastry and place on the centre of each pastry rectangle.

Brush the pastry on one side of the sausagemeat with the beaten egg, and fold the other side of the pastry over onto the egg-washed edge. Press down to seal and trim any excess. Cut each pastry roll into 4 large sausage rolls or 8 mini rolls with a sharp knife.

Place the sausage rolls on a baking sheet, and bake in the oven for 15–20 minutes until the pastry is puffed, crisp, and golden and the sausagemeat is completely cooked through. Serve hot or cold.

*Tip*

**Try adding grated Granny Smith apples or finely chopped apricots for fruity sausage rolls.**

# Main Courses

Making the most of ingredients such as potatoes, rice noodles, pulses and gluten-free pasta, this chapter offers a huge range of robust, hearty and flavourful dishes, including a Lamb Shank Pie which is perfect for a dinner party and family favourites such as pizzas and fish pie.

# PIZZAS

**The best thing about making pizzas at home is that you can choose your own topping. Get your kids creating something colourful with different ingredients. Here are delicious ideas to get you started.**

## CHEESY BACON, ONION & POTATO PIZZA

**This topping is rich and warming, and evocative of Alpine tartiflette. Waxy potato varieties such as Charlotte or Vivaldi work best. Serve with a simple green salad.**

SERVES 4

- 560 g medium waxy potatoes
- 1 tbsp extra virgin olive oil
- 200 g smoky bacon lardons or pancetta
- 2 medium onions, thinly sliced
- 2 large garlic cloves, finely chopped
- 2 tbsp dry white wine
- 300 g mascarpone cheese
- 4 x 20–25 cm gluten-free thin-crust pizza bases
- 40 g grated Emmental or Gruyère cheese
- 1 tbsp finely grated Parmesan cheese
- 1 tbsp fresh thyme leaves
- salt and freshly ground black pepper

First, boil the potatoes until just tender in the centre when tested with a sharp knife. Drain, then leave to cool and thinly slice.

Preheat the oven to 200°C.

Heat the olive oil in a frying pan, and fry the lardons until light golden. Transfer to a bowl.

Using the reserved bacon fat, gently fry the onions, seasoned with pepper, until soft and golden. Add the garlic and fry for a further 30 seconds. Pour in the wine and boil until the liquid is reduced by half. Add the onion and wine mixture to the bacon, and stir in the mascarpone cheese. Season with salt and pepper.

Place the 4 pizza bases on to 2 large baking sheets. Spoon on the mascarpone mixture and spread out thinly and evenly over the bases. Arrange the potato slices on top, then sprinkle with the Emmenthal and a large pinch of the Parmesan.

Sprinkle with the thyme, and season with a little black pepper. Bake in the oven for 20 minutes, or until the cheese topping is golden and bubbling. Serve immediately.

## AMERICAN HOT BEEF & PEPPER PIZZA

**This pizza topping is often out of bounds for gluten-free pizza lovers in restaurants due to the spice and rusk mix added to the meat, so try this delicious recipe in the comfort of your own home.**

**SERVES 4**

- 2 medium onions, thinly sliced
- 1 red pepper, deseeded and cut in 1-cm dice
- 2 tbsp extra virgin olive oil
- 2 garlic cloves, finely chopped
- pinch of chilli flakes
- 1 fresh long green chilli, deseeded and finely sliced
- 1 tsp ground cumin
- 1 tsp ground coriander
- 1 tsp oregano, dried, plus 1 tbsp for sprinkling
- 400 g lean beef mince
- 4 x 20–25 cm gluten-free pizza bases
- 1 quantity Italian Tomato Sauce (page 99)
- 2 balls of buffalo mozzarella cheese, thinly sliced
- salt and freshly ground black pepper

Preheat the oven to 200°C.

In a frying pan, gently fry the onions and red pepper in 1 tablespoon of the olive oil, lightly seasoned with salt and pepper, until soft. Add the garlic, chilli flakes, green chilli, cumin, coriander and the 1 tsp of oregano, and fry for a further 30 seconds. Tip the spiced onion mixture into a bowl. Set aside.

Heat the remaining oil in the same pan. When hot, add the beef mince, and season with salt and pepper. Fry, stirring regularly, for 10 minutes, or until browned. Return the onion mixture to the pan with the meat, stir through, and remove from the heat.

Spread the tomato sauce over the pizza bases, then top with the spicy beef mixture.

Arrange the mozzarella slices on top, and season with pepper and a light sprinkling of oregano.

Bake in the oven for 20 minutes, or until the crust is golden and the cheese is melted and bubbling. Serve immediately.

## TRICOLOR PESTO, MOZZARELLA & CHERRY TOMATO PIZZA

**A colourful pizza topping with ripe fresh tomatoes and freshly made basil pesto. Try making this pizza with rocket and walnut pesto, and scattered with rocket leaves, as a variation.**

**SERVES 4**

- 4 x 20–25-cm gluten-free pizza bases
- 1 quantity freshly-made Basil and Pine Nut Pesto or a good-quality jar of gluten-free pesto
- 2 x 125g balls buffalo mozzarella, thinly sliced
- 300 g ripe cherry tomatoes, halved
- extra virgin olive oil for drizzling
- salt and freshly ground black pepper
- at least 5 fresh basil leaves per pizza, to garnish

Preheat the oven to 200°C.

Place the 4 pizza bases on large baking sheets.

Evenly spread the pesto over the pizza bases, then arrange the mozzarella slices on top. Drizzle with olive oil, and season with salt and pepper.

Bake in the oven for 15 minutes, or until the mozzarella is golden brown and bubbling. Scatter over the cherry tomatoes and basil leaves, and serve immediately.

# SAUCES

**Smooth sauces for stews and gravies, creamy béchamel sauce and cheese sauce are made by thickening cooking liquors, stock and milk with a paste called a roux. A roux is traditionally made with an equal quantity of wheat flour and fat such as melted butter, dripping or oil. Both cornflour and rice flour stand in very well for wheat flour.**

## BÉCHAMEL SAUCE

This classic aromatic white sauce, subtly flavoured with onion, bay leaves, peppercorns and nutmeg, adds a light creaminess to lasagne, moussaka and fish pie, and forms the base for cheese, mushroom and parsley sauce. Traditionally made with whole dairy milk, béchamel sauce tastes just as good made with dairy-free soya milk.

**MALES 500 ML**

- 500 ml whole milk or dairy-free soya milk
- 1 bay leaf
- ½ onion, thickly sliced
- pinch of freshly grated nutmeg
- large pinch of salt
- 2 grinds of fresh black pepper
- 25 g butter or vegetable oil
- 25 g cornflour or rice flour

Pour the milk into a large pan, then add the bay leaf, onion, nutmeg, salt and pepper. Gently bring to a simmer. Remove from the heat and leave to stand for 30 minutes to allow the flavours to infuse.

In a separate pan, melt the butter or heat the oil, then remove the pan from the heat and stir in the cornflour or rice flour to form a smooth paste called a roux. Return to the heat and cook the roux for 1 minute to remove the raw flour flavour.

Strain the milk, discarding the flavourings and stir 100 ml into the roux off the heat. Once the paste is smooth again, add another 100 ml milk and stir until smooth.

Return the roux to a medium heat, and gradually stir in the rest of the milk. Continue to stirring the sauce until it reaches simmering point and thickens to the consistency of runny yoghurt. Continue to stir for a further 2 minutes to cook out the flour. The sauce should be smooth and glossy. Remove from the heat and use as needed.

**FOR CHEESE SAUCE**

To freshly made hot béchamel sauce, stir in 80 g of grated mature Cheddar cheese and 15 g finely grated parmesan. Taste and season with salt and freshly ground black pepper if necessary. Use as a base for our family-friendly dishes, including cauliflower and macaroni cheese, or spooned over poached, firm white fish.

**FOR PARSLEY SAUCE**

Add 1 tablespoon of finely chopped parsley to 1 quantity of béchamel sauce, and season to taste with salt and freshly ground black pepper. Serve with fishcakes, gammon, smoked and white fish or poached chicken.

# LASAGNE AL FORNO

**Lasagne, particularly the version originating from Bologna, is synonymous with warmth and comfort. This recipe makes a delicious gluten-free lasagne that I guarantee everyone will devour, accompanied by a lightly dressed green salad.**

- SERVES 4–6

- FOR THE RAGÙ

3–4 tbsp light olive oil
500 g lean beef mince
500 g lean pork mince
1 large onion, finely diced
2 celery sticks, finely diced
3 medium carrots, finely diced
2 large garlic cloves, finely chopped
2 large thyme sprigs
2 bay leaves
1 tbsp, finely chopped fresh oregano leaves
250 ml red wine
3 x 400 g tinned chopped tomatoes
250 ml chicken or vegetable stock
500 ml quantity of béchamel sauce
salt and freshly ground black pepper

- FOR THE LASAGNE

12–15 gluten-free lasagne
4 tbsp grated Parmesan
250 g buffalo mozzarella, thinly sliced

Firstly, make the ragù. In a large pan, brown the beef mince seasoned with salt and pepper in half the olive oil, then transfer to a large bowl. Add the pork mince to the pan, season with salt and pepper and brown in the remaining fat. Add to the bowl with cooked beef mince.

Add another 1 tablespoon of olive oil to the pan, and gently fry the onion, celery and carrots, covered with a lid, until softened and golden. Add the garlic and herbs, and gently fry for a further minute.

Return the browned beef and pork, including any juices, to the pan with the vegetables. Stir in the wine, tomatoes and stock. If needed, add more water to cover. Bring to the simmer over a medium heat, and gently cook, uncovered, for 1½ hours, or until the meat is very tender and the sauce has thickened. Skim off any fat that rises to the surface. Taste and season with salt and pepper if needed.

Preheat the oven to 200°C.

Make the béchamel sauce following the instructions on page 86 and mix into the ragù.

To assemble the lasagne, spread a third of the sauce evenly over the bottom of a lasagne dish, sprinkle with a third of the Parmesan and cover with 4 or 5 pasta sheets. Spread another third of sauce over the pasta sheets and sprinkle on the second third of Parmesan. Add another layer of pasta, spread on the remaining sauce and cover with the mozzarella. Sprinkle over the remaining grated Parmesan.

Place the lasagne dish in a shallow roasting tin, and bake the lasagne in the oven for 30 minutes until the top is golden and the sauce is bubbling around the edge of the dish.

To serve, use a sharp knife to slice the lasagne into 6 portions, and serve immediately on warm plates.

**Replace the meat with bite-sized roasted vegetables of your choice.**

# FISH PIE WITH CRUNCHY CHEESE TOPPING

- SERVES 6

450 g skinned salmon fillet
450 g skinned haddock fillet
500 ml whole milk or dairy-free milk
½ large onion, sliced
2 bay leaves
large pinch of salt
4 grinds of black pepper
4 hard-boiled eggs, quartered
1 tbsp finely chopped flat-leaf parsley
30 g butter or dairy-free margarine
30 g cornflour
seasoned mashed potato made with 900 g peeled potatoes, 70 g butter or dairy-free margarine, 100 ml milk or dairy-free milk and salt and freshly ground black pepper

- FOR THE CRUNCHY CHEESE TOPPING

3 slices white bread, whizzed to breadcrumbs
1 tbsp grated Parmesan or mature Cheddar cheese
3 grinds of black pepper
2 tbsp olive oil

**Fish pie is the ultimate comfort food, enjoyed by all ages and often by those who do not usually enjoy fish. The cheesy crumble adds texture and flavour to this warming dish.**

Preheat the oven to 180°C.

Arrange the fish fillets in the bottom of a large ovenproof dish.

Cover the fish with the milk and sprinkle over the onion. Add the bay leaves and season with salt and pepper. Cover the dish with foil and bake in the oven for 20 minutes, or until the fish is just cooked through.

Strain off the milk and reserve for making the sauce.

Break the fish into bite-sized pieces, and arrange in the bottom of a clean, deep ovenproof dish.

Add the eggs and sprinkle over the parsley.

To make the sauce, in a small pan, melt the butter, stir in the cornflour and remove from the heat. Gradually stir in the strained milk, being careful to mix out the lumps before adding each splash of milk.

Return the sauce to a medium heat, and stir until the sauce thickens and begins to boil. Taste and adjust the season as needed.

Pour the sauce over the fish and eggs.

Spoon the mashed potato over the fish mixture, and spread out with a fork until all the fish is covered.

To make the topping, mix the breadcrumbs, cheese and black pepper together, and sprinkle evenly over the mashed potato. Drizzle the olive oil all over the pie.

Bake the pie in the oven on a baking sheet for 20 minutes until the potato and topping is golden brown and crisp. Serve immediately.

**If you are cooking for someone who needs a dairy-free diet, replace dairy milk with soya milk and use 1 tablespoon of thyme leaves in the topping instead of cheese.**

# MOROCCAN-SPICED CAULIFLOWER CHEESE

- SERVES 4

1 large head of cauliflower, cut into bite-sized florets
2 tbsp olive oil
1 onion, thinly sliced
2 tsp cumin seeds
1 tsp coriander seeds
1 medium red chilli, deseeded and finely sliced
2 garlic cloves, finely chopped
2 quantities (1 litre) cheese sauce (page 86)
2 tbsp gluten-free white breadcrumbs
40 g mature Cheddar cheese, grated
salt and freshly ground black pepper

**This spicy twist on a classic dish is simply delicious! Serve with cold meats or a green salad and boiled new potatoes.**

Preheat the oven to 200°C.

Steam or boil the cauliflower florets for 5 minutes, or until just tender. Remove from the heat, drain and leave to steam dry.

In a frying pan, heat the oil over a medium heat. With a pinch of salt and black pepper, fry the onion until soft and golden. Add 1 tsp of the cumin seeds, coriander seeds, chilli and garlic to the pan. Cook, stirring, over the heat for 30 seconds. Stir the spiced onion mixture into the cheese sauce. Gently mix the cauliflower into the cheese sauce, and pour into a baking dish.

Mix the breadcrumbs with the grated Cheddar cheese, remaining cumin seeds and 2 grinds of pepper. Sprinkle over the cauliflower cheese. Bake in the oven for 20–25 minutes until golden brown and crispy on top and bubbling hot around the edges.

# MACARONI CHEESE

- SERVES 4–6

250 g gluten-free macaroni pasta
2 x quantities cheese sauce (page 86)
210 g mature Cheddar, grated
50 g grated Parmesan
freshly ground black pepper

*Tip*

**Gluten-free macaroni is available in specialist and larger stores, but if you cannot find it use penne or fusilli to make this dish.**

**This simple dish seems to represent comfort food across the English-speaking world and, amazingly, escapes the addition of local ingredients in preference of a pure cheesy flavour.**

Preheat the oven to 200°C.

Cook the pasta as per the packet instructions until just soft. Drain well and set aside.

Make the cheese sauce and stir in 120 g of the Cheddar cheese while the sauce is hot. Season with pepper.

Stir the cooked pasta into the sauce, and transfer to a deep ovenproof dish.

Sprinkle over the remaining Cheddar and the Parmesan and place the dish in the oven. Bake for 15 minutes until the cheese is golden and bubbling. Serve immediately.

# SALMON, CHIVE & LEMON FISHCAKES SERVED WITH TARTARE SAUCE

**A real friend and family pleaser! You can't go wrong serving fish cakes. These colourful and tasty fishcakes taste at their best served straight from the pan, simply with tartare sauce, garden peas and a wedge of lemon. In place of the tartare sauce, serve the fishcakes with parsley sauce (page 86).**

- SERVES 4

500 g floury potatoes, peeled and diced
450 g salmon fillet, skin left on
570 ml milk or dairy-free milk
1 bay leaf
1 small onion, sliced
30 g butter or dairy-free margarine
1 egg, beaten
½ tbsp finely snipped chives
zest of 1 lemon
140 g gluten-free white bread, whizzed into breadcrumbs
4 tbsp sflower oil, for frying
salt and freshly ground black pepper

- FOR THE TARTARE SAUCE

4 tbsp mayonnaise
1 tbsp capers rinsed, drained and finely chopped
1 tbsp gherkins, rinsed and drained, finely chopped
1 small onion, finely chopped
1 tbsp finely chopped curly parsley
squeeze of lemon
salt and freshly ground black pepper

First, simmer the potatoes in gently boiling salted water for 20 minutes, or until tender. Drain and steam dry.

Place the salmon skin-side down in a frying pan. Pour the milk over the fillets. If the fillets are exposed, add some more milk or water to cover. Add the bay leaf, onion and 4 grinds of black pepper. Bring the milk slowly to a simmer, and gently poach the fish for 10 minutes, or until the fish is just cooked through. Reserve the poaching milk.

To make the tartare sauce, mix all the ingredients together and season with salt and pepper. Spoon into a serving bowl.

Mash the potatoes with 1–2 tablespoons of the poaching milk and the butter.

Separate the flakes of salmon from the skin and mix with the mashed potatoes, egg, chives and lemon zest. The mixture should be firm enough to hold its shape. Add an additional 1–2 tablespoons of poaching milk if the mixture is too stiff. Taste and adjust the seasoning as needed.

Using wet hands to prevent the mixture sticking and shape the salmon mixture into 8 round flat cakes no more than 2.5 cm thick. Coat the fishcakes with breadcrumbs, then brush off any loose crumbs.

Heat the oil in the frying pan over a medium heat. When the oil is hot, place 4 fish cakes at a time into the pan and fry until golden brown on both sides. Remove from the pan and keep warm in a low oven while the remaining cakes are fried.

*Tip*

**Use floury potatoes such as King Edward or Maris Piper.**

# PORK ESCALOPES WITH LEMON, GARLIC & ROSEMARY

**The tenderness and delicate flavour of pork fillet contrasts beautifully with the crisp herby breadcrumb coating. Serve these delicious escalopes with a lightly dressed green salad.**

- SERVES 4

4 slices gluten-free white bread, whizzed into fine breadcrumbs
zest of 1 lemon
2 garlic cloves, finely chopped
1 tbsp finely chopped rosemary
2 tbsp cornflour, seasoned with salt and freshly ground black pepper
4 x 100 g pork fillet slices
2 eggs, beaten
3 tbsp light olive oil
salt and freshly ground black pepper

Blend the breadcrumbs, lemon zest, garlic and rosemary in a food processor until well mixed. Season with salt and pepper, and spread over the bottom of a large, shallow dish.

Sprinkle the seasoned cornflour over the bottom of a separate dish, and pour the beaten egg into another.

For the pork escalopes, first place the pork fillets between 2 sheets of greaseproof paper, then use a rolling pin or the base of a pan to flatten to 3 mm thick. Next, press both sides of each pork escalope in the flour, cover in beaten egg and finally coat both sides in the breadcrumb mixture. Gently shake each breaded escalope to remove any loose crumbs, and place on a large dish ready for frying.

Heat the olive oil in a large ovenproof frying pan. Fry 2 pork escalopes at a time, for 4–5 minutes on each side until the breadcrumb crust is golden and crisp, and the juices run clear when the pork is pierced with a skewer. Serve immediately.

# ROAST CHICKEN WITH MUSHROOM, LEMON, GARLIC, PROSCIUTTO & HERB STUFFING

- SERVES 4

- FOR THE STUFFING

1 onion, finely diced
110 g chestnut mushrooms, finely sliced
2 tbsp light olive oil
70 g prosciutto slices, roughly chopped
2 garlic cloves, finely chopped
1 tbsp flat-leaf parsley, finely chopped
1 tbsp thyme leaves
finely grated zest of 1 lemon and juice of ½ lemon
5 slices gluten-free white bread whizzed to breadcrumbs
salt and freshly ground black pepper

- FOR THE CHICKEN

1 x 1.5-kg free range chicken
2 tbsp extra virgin olive oil
1 tbsp cornflour
200 ml chicken stock
200 ml white wine
2 thyme sprigs
salt and freshly ground black pepper

**Roast chicken is fail-safe and is transformed into a truly special meal with this flavoursome stuffing. For a richer, more seasonal stuffing, replace this lemon and prosciutto stuffing with the Chestnut and Apricot Sausagemeat Stuffing (see opposite).**

Preheat the oven to 200°C.

In a pan over a medium heat, gently fry the onion and mushrooms, seasoned with salt and pepper, in the olive oil until soft and sweet. Add the prosciutto, garlic, parsley and thyme leaves, and continue to fry gently for a further minute. Stir in the lemon zest and juice and breadcrumbs. Taste and season again with salt and pepper if needed, then remove from the heat.

Season the cavity of the chicken with salt and pepper, before placing it in a roasting tin. Spoon the stuffing into the chicken cavity. Drizzle the olive oil over the chicken, season with salt and pepper, and roast in the oven for 1½ hours until the juices between the thighs and breast run clear.

To make the gravy, lift the chicken out of the roasting tray onto a serving plate. Cover with foil. Put the roasting dish over a medium heat, stir the cornflour into the fat and juices, then add the chicken stock, white wine and thyme. Bring the liquid to the boil, stirring all the time and scraping any browned bits away from the bottom and sides of the dish into the gravy. When the gravy has thickened, remove from the heat.

To serve, thinly slice the chicken and serve on warm plates with a spoonful of stuffing and gravy.

*Tip*

**Try replacing the breadcrumbs with cooked white or brown rice for a more substantial stuffing.**

# APRICOT & CHESTNUT SAUSAGEMEAT STUFFING

**This fruity and aromatic stuffing recipe has been handed down through my family for the past three generations at least, and Christmas lunch is not complete without it. You can also use this stuffing to add richness and succulence to roast chicken or a rolled joint of pork. The gravy made from the cooking juices is divine. The recipe is for a 5.5-kg oven-ready turkey and can be assembled a day in advance. Halve the quantity of ingredients to make stuffing for a large roast chicken or rolled pork joint.**

- SERVES 4

1½ onions, very finely diced
2 celery sticks, finely diced
4 garlic cloves, finely chopped
2 tbsp vegetable oil
450 g minced pork belly
400 g tinned unsweetened chestnut purée
4 slices gluten-free white or brown bread, whizzed into fine breadcrumbs
1 tbsp finely chopped thyme
1 tsbp finely chopped sage
1 tbsp finely chopped curly parsley
110 g dried ready-to-eat apricots, roughly chopped
2 tsp fine salt and 8 grinds of black pepper
2 medium eggs, beaten

Place the onion and celery in a pan with the oil. Season with salt and pepper, and gently fry, covered, until the onion is very soft and sweet. Add the garlic and fry, stirring constantly, for a further 30 seconds. Remove from the heat and leave to cool.

When cold, tip the softened onion mixture into a large bowl with all of the remaining ingredients and mix together thoroughly with your hands.

To check that the stuffing is well seasoned, fry a flattened spoonful of the mixture in a little hot oil until it is cooked through. Taste and add more seasoning to the mixture as needed.

Use some of the stuffing to loosely stuff the neck end of the turkey, cover with the skin flap and secure with a skewer. Flatten the remaining stuffing in a shallow ovenproof dish, and bake for 30 minutes at 200°C.

# MINI HOMEMADE SAUSAGES SERVED WITH CABBAGE, APPLE & TOASTED WALNUT SLAW

- SERVES 4

- FOR THE SLAW

50g walnuts, roughly chopped
90 ml cider vinegar
2 tsp runny honey
1 heaped tsp grainy mustard
2 tbsp extra virgin olive oil
1 tbsp walnut oil
400 g white cabbage, shredded
1 Granny Smith apple, coarsely grated
1 carrot, coarsely grated
4 spring onions, thinly sliced on the diagonal
salt and freshly ground black pepper

- FOR THE SAUSAGES

450 g minced pork belly
½ onion, very finely diced
½ Granny Smith apple, peeled, quartered, cored and coarsely grated
2 tbsp gluten-free white breadcrumbs
1 tbsp finely chopped thyme
1 tbsp finely chopped sage
1 tbsp finely chopped curly parsley
1 garlic clove, finely chopped
1 tsp salt and 5 grinds of freshly ground black pepper
vegetable oil for frying

**Homemade sausages have a more interesting flavour and meatier texture than ready-made sausages, but for a speedy meal there is a good choice of gluten-free sausages available. The slaw is also ideal to serve with grilled or barbecued meat and poultry.**

First, prepare the cabbage slaw. Lightly toast the walnuts in a dry frying pan over a medium heat for 2 minutes.

In a large bowl, mix the cider vinegar, honey and mustard together. Season with salt and pepper, then whisk in the olive and walnut oils.

Add the cabbage, apple, carrot, spring onions and walnuts to the bowl, and mix thoroughly with the dressing. Cover and leave to stand while you make the sausages.

Place all the sausagemeat ingredients together in a bowl, season well with salt and pepper, and mix together thoroughly with your hands.

To check that the sausagemeat is well seasoned, fry a small, flattened spoonful of the mixture in some hot oil until cooked thoroughly and golden brown on both sides. Taste and, if needed, mix in more salt and pepper.

With wet hands, shape the sausagemeat into 16 even-sized baby sausages or 8 larger sausages.

Gently fry the sausages in hot oil, turning them frequently until the sausages are cooked through and golden brown all over. This should take about 10 minutes.

Serve the sausages with the cabbage slaw on the side.

*Tip*

**This sausagemeat recipe makes a great stuffing for roast chicken and the Christmas turkey.**

# BRAISED MEATBALLS WITH TOMATO SAUCE & GREEN OLIVES & SOFT PARMESAN POLENTA

- SERVES 4–6

750 g pork mince
2 garlic cloves, crushed
1 tbsp chopped oregano leaves
1 tbsp chopped flat-lraf parsley leaves
2 tbsp fresh white breadcrumbs
1 egg, lightly beaten
salt and freshly ground black pepper

- FOR THE SAUCE

1 quantity Italian Tomato Sauce (see opposite)
½ red chilli, finely chopped
150 g pitted green olives

- FOR THE POLENTA

750 ml chicken stock, or the equivalent quoted on the pack
200 g instant polenta
30 g Parmesan, finely grated
40 g butter, diced
salt and freshly ground black pepper

**This gutsy Italian dish is the ultimate comfort food for an informal meal. As an alternative to polenta, serve the meatballs with rice or gluten-free pasta.**

First, make the sauce, adding the red chilli to the frying vegetables. Set aside.

To make the meatballs, combine the mince, garlic, herbs, breadcrumbs, seasoning and egg in a bowl. Fry a small quantity of the mixture until golden brown on each side. Taste and adjust the seasoning with salt and pepper as needed. Roll level tablespoons of the mixture into balls with wet hands. Place on a plate in a single layer.

Heat half the oil in a large pan, and gently fry the meatballs in batches until golden brown.

Stir the Italian tomato and chilli sauce and the olives into the meatballs. Simmer gently, uncovered, for 10–15 minutes until the meatballs are cooked through.

Meanwhile, make the polenta by bringing the chicken stock to the boil in a medium pan. Pour the polenta into the stock in a thin, steady stream, whisking continuously. Continue to whisk the polenta for 4–5 minutes while the polenta simmers and until the stock has been fully absorbed; the thickened polenta should fall cleanly away from the sides of the pan. Stir in the Parmesan and butter, and season with salt and pepper.

To serve, place a generous spoonful of polenta on each of 4 warm plates, followed by the meatballs and lots of sauce. Serve with freshly grated Parmesan.

# ITALIAN TOMATO SAUCE

**The rich sweet and sour flavours in Italian Tomato Sauce lift a simple bowl of pasta, provide a tasty base for pizza toppings and add colour and zing to vegetables, baked dishes, meat, fish and poultry. Using a mixture of ripe fresh tomato and tinned tomato, and aromatic vegetables gives a fresh balanced flavour.**

- SERVES 4

2 tbsp extra virgin olive oil
1 celery stick, diced
1 large onion, diced
2 medium carrots, diced
1 garlic clove
400 g ripe vine tomatoes, diced
400 g tinned chopped tomatoes
1 large thyme sprig
salt and freshly ground black pepper

In a large pan, heat the olive oil over a medium heat, and gently fry the celery, onion and carrot until soft with a pinch of salt and 2 or 3 grinds of pepper. Stir in the garlic and fry for a further 30 seconds.

Add the fresh and tinned tomatoes and thyme to the softened vegetables, and bring to the simmer. Simmer in an uncovered pan for 30 minutes, or until the sauce thickens to coating consistency. Taste and season again if needed before serving or using as part of another recipe.

## SAUCE VARIATIONS

**Like a béchamel, Italian tomato sauce provides a base for other flavours. For smooth sauces, whiz until smooth in a food processor. Here are some variations on a theme:**

### FOR TOMATO AND BACON SAUCE

Fry 75 g smoked bacon lardons or thinly sliced streaky bacon rashers in 1 tablespoon of olive oil until crisp and golden. Stir into 1 quantity of Italian Tomato Sauce, and serve with pasta or with meat, poultry or firm white fish. This sauce is also good spiced up with finely sliced red chilli fried with the vegetables.

### FOR TOMATO AND BUTTER SAUCE

For a rich-tasting sauce, replace the olive oil in the recipe for Italian Tomato Sauce above with 50 g butter.

### FOR TOMATO WITH GARLIC AND BASIL

Add 3 extra garlic cloves to the recipe for Italian Tomato Sauce above. When the sauce is cooked, stir in a handful of finely torn basil.

# BAKED PENNE WITH MUSHROOM & THYME SAUCE

- SERVES 4

1 litre milk or dairy-free milk
30 g dried wild mushrooms
2 bay leaves
2 thyme sprigs
70 g butter or dairy-free margarine
1 onion, thinly sliced
150 g fresh chestnut or wild mushrooms, sliced
2 garlic cloves, finely chopped
40 g cornflour
400 g gluten-free penne pasta
4 tbsp freshly grated Parmesan or dairy-free – breadcrumbs mixed with 1 tablespoon thyme leaves, plus extra, to serve
salt and freshly ground black pepper

**A rich and comforting recipe designed to make informal catering easy. Serve from the baking dish with a green salad and a glass of wine. Sit back and enjoy.**

Preheat the oven to 190°C.

Place the milk, dried mushrooms, bay leaves and thyme in a pan, season with pepper and bring to boiling point. Remove from the heat, and leave to stand for 30 minutes to allow the flavours to infuse. Strain the flavoured milk into a bowl, retaining the mushrooms.

Melt the butter or dairy-free margarine in a clean pan, and gently fry the onion and fresh mushrooms, seasoned with salt and pepper, over a low heat until soft. Add the garlic and fry for 30 seconds. Stir in the cornflour to make a roux, cook for 30 seconds, then remove from the heat.

Gradually stir the mushroom-flavoured milk and reserved wild mushrooms into the roux, to form a smooth paste. Return the pan to a medium heat, and stir the sauce continuously until it thickens to a light coating consistency. Taste and season with salt and pepper as needed. Set aside.

Meanwhile, cook the pasta in a large pan of boiling salted water as per the pack instructions, or until tender. Drain in a colander, pour into a large bowl and gently stir in the mushroom sauce.

Pour the pasta mixture into a lightly greased 2-litre ovenproof dish, and spread out evenly. Sprinkle the grated Parmesan (or herby breadcrumbs) over the pasta, and bake in the oven for 30–40 minutes until the sauce is bubbling around the edges and the top is golden brown.

Serve from the dish at the table onto warm plates with extra Parmesan if using.

*Tip*

**For a meatier variation, stir 200 g smoked bacon lardons, fried until golden brown, or sliced chicken breast, into the cooked pasta with the mushroom sauce, before baking in the oven.**

# PASTA WITH BRAISED PEAS, SMOKED BACON, SPRING ONION & MINT

**This is a really good last-minute dish using kitchen cupboard staples, particularly when food shopping is overdue. This dish tastes rich and luxurious with the addition of crème fraîche but is just as good without.**

- SERVES 4–6

400 g gluten-free fusilli or penne pasta
1 tbsp extra virgin olive oil

- FOR THE SAUCE

2 tbsp extra virgin olive oil
220 g smoked bacon lardons or streaky bacon rashers, thinly sliced across into strips
1 bunch of spring onions, finely sliced
2 garlic cloves, finely chopped
300 g frozen garden peas
1 tbsp roughly chopped mint
2 heaped tbsp crème fraîche (optional)
salt and freshly ground black pepper
freshly grated Parmesan cheese, to serve

Cook the pasta in boiling salted water as per the pack instruction, or until the pasta is tender. Drain, return to the pan and stir in the 1 tablespoon olive oil. Cover with a lid and set aside.

Meanwhile, make the sauce. In a large pan, heat the oil and fry the bacon until crisp and golden. Add the spring onions and garlic, and cook for a further minute. Tip the frozen peas into the pan, cover with a lid and braise for 10 minutes. Stir in the mint and cook for 1 minute. Remove from the heat, and stir in the crème fraîche, if using. Taste and season lightly with salt and pepper, if needed.

Pour the bacon and pea sauce over the cooked pasta, and toss together until well mixed.

Spoon into warm bowls, sprinkle over the Parmesan and serve immediately.

# PASTA WITH CRAB, CHILLI AND ROCKET

- SERVES 4

400 g gluten-free fusilli or penne pasta
5 tbsp extra virgin olive oil
3 garlic cloves, finely chopped
1 long fresh red chilli, deseeded and finely chopped
250 g cooked white crabmeat
grated zest and juice of 1 lemon
2 large handfuls of rocket leaves
large pinch of salt and freshly ground black pepper
4 lemon wedges to garnish

**This light, subtle and summery pasta dish makes a great meal with a crisp green salad. Try making it with prawns too.**

Cook the pasta in boiling salted water as per the pack instructions, or until tender. Drain, then stir in 1 tablespoon of the olive oil. Cover and set aside while you prepare the crab sauce.

To make the sauce, heat the remaining oil in a medium pan over a medium heat. Add the garlic and chilli, and gently fry for 30 seconds, then stir in the crabmeat, lemon zest and juice, and rocket leaves. Season the sauce with salt and pepper, and gently heat through for 1–2 minutes.

Pour the sauce into the cooked pasta and stir well.

Serve immediately with extra olive oil for drizzling and the lemon wedges.

## ROCKET & WALNUT PESTO

**A punchy, peppery sauce to serve with pasta, on pizzas and tossed into a potato or pasta salad. Although this pesto can be stored in a sealed container in the fridge for up to 2 days, it tastes at its best and most vibrant eaten just after it is made.**

**SERVES 4**

- 70 g rocket, rinsed under cold, running water and dried
- 2 garlic cloves, roughly chopped
- 50 g walnuts, roughly chopped
- 5 tbsp extra virgin olive oil
- 70 g Parmesan cheese, grated (optional)
- salt and freshly ground black pepper

Place all the ingredients in a food processor, season with salt and pepper, and blend until smooth.

# CHICKEN & PRAWN PAD THAI

**This traditional Thai stir-fried noodle dish is full of complex flavours and textures. It is also very moreish, so beware!**

Mix the fish sauce with the tamarind paste and sugar in a small bowl, and set aside. Toast the peanuts in a dry frying pan until golden brown. Chop roughly and set aside.

Heat a large wok over a high heat. Add the oil and, when hot, stir-fry the sliced chicken for 4–5 minutes until it is cooked through. Add the prawns, garlic and shallots, and cook for 1 minute, or until the prawns are hot. Add the shrimp paste and chilli and stir-fry for 30 seconds.

Add the noodles to the pan, and stir-fry with the other ingredients until heated through. Drizzle in the egg and stir through the fried noodles until just set.

Stir in the fish sauce and tamarind mixture, beansprouts and half the chopped peanuts. Cook for 1 minute, or until the sprouts start to wilt. Taste and add a little more fish sauce or sugar, if needed.

To serve, heap the pad thai into warm bowls, and top with the remaining chopped peanuts, beansprouts, coriander leaves, spring onions and lime wedges.

Serve immediately with a small bowl of fish sauce spiced up with finely sliced red chilli.

*Tip*

**Ready-cooked Thai rice noodles, shrimp paste, fish sauce and tamarind paste are available in good supermarkets and Asian supermarkets.**

- SERVES 4

2 tbsp fish sauce
2 tbsp tamarind paste
1 tbsp soft brown sugar
80 g unsalted peanuts
4 tbsp vegetable or groundnut oil
4 chicken breasts, thinly sliced across
100 g medium cooked and peeled prawns
4 garlic cloves, finely chopped
3 shallots, finely sliced
1 tsp Thai dried shrimp paste
1–2 long red chillies, deseeded and finely sliced
600 g ready-cooked Thai ribbon rice noodles
3 eggs, lightly beaten
large handful of beansprouts
salt and freshly ground black pepper

- TO SERVE

large handful roughly chopped coriander leaves
handful of beansprouts
4 spring onions, finely sliced on the diagonal
1 lime, cut into 4 wedges
1 fresh red chilli, deseeded and finely sliced, mixed with 100 ml fish sauce

# CHICKEN BIRYANI

- SERVES 4

- FOR THE CHICKEN MARINADE

2 tsp coriander seeds
2 tsp cumin seeds
1 tsp chilli flakes
½ tsp ground cinnamon
½ tsp ground turmeric
½ tsp finely grated nutmeg
4 garlic cloves, finely chopped
3-cm piece of fresh root ginger, peeled and finely chopped
250 ml natural yoghurt or plain dairy-free yoghurt
8 chicken thigh fillets, cut into 3

- FOR THE RICE

400 g basmati rice
1 tsp salt
2 tbsp vegetable oil
2 large onions, thinly sliced
2 bay leaves
4 cardamom pods
2 tsp soft dark brown sugar
4 handfuls of raisins
1 cinnamon stick
400 ml tinned coconut milk

- FOR THE RAITA

½ cucumber, deseeded and coarsely grated
300 ml natural yoghurt or plain dairy-free yoghurt
large handful of mint leaves, finely sliced

- FOR THE GARNISH

handful coriander leaves, roughly chopped
4 lemon wedges

**An aromatic and satisfying family-friendly Indian celebration dish, originating in Persia. Serve with cucumber raita, fresh coriander and lemon wedges.**

First, prepare the chicken marinade. Toast the coriander and cumin seeds in a dry frying pan until aromatic, being careful not to burn them. Remove the pan from the heat, and stir in the chilli flakes and ready-ground spices. Grind to a fine powder with a mortar and pestle. Pour the ground spices into a large bowl, and mix with the garlic, ginger and yoghurt. Turn the chicken over in the marinade, cover and leave to marinate in the fridge overnight.

To prepare the rice, place in a sieve and rinse under a cold, running tap until the water runs clear, then place in a large pan. Cover with cold water to 2 cm above the top of the rice. Add the salt and bring to a simmer. Reduce the heat to the lowest setting, then cover with a lid and cook for 20 minutes, or until the water has been absorbed and pitting appears on the surface of the rice.

Meanwhile, heat 1 tablespoon of the oil in a frying pan over a medium heat, and fry the onions for 5 minutes, or until golden brown. Transfer the onions to a dish and add the remaining oil to the pan. Lift the chicken out of the marinade, and fry over a medium heat until cooked through and golden brown on all sides. Reduce the heat and stir in the marinade with the bay leaves, cardamom, sugar, raisins, cooked rice, cinnamon stick and coconut milk. Cover the pan with a tight-fitting lid and gently heat for 10 minutes, or until piping hot.

To make the raita, mix the ingredients together and transfer to a serving bowl.

To serve, pile the biryani onto warm plates and sprinkle with coriander, Serve with wedges of lemon and the raita.

# GOAN SEAFOOD CURRY

**I first tasted this delicate and very special seafood curry in a Goan beach café during my gap year, many moons ago – and I can still taste it! Flavoured with warm notes of mixed spice and cinnamon, this is best served simply with fresh coriander, fluffy basmati rice and a wedge of lemon.**

- SERVES 4

2 tsp coriander seeds
2 tsp cumin seeds
1 tsp ground cinnamon
½ tsp ground mixed spice
large pinch of salt
1½ tbsp vegetable oil
1 large onion, thinly sliced
5-cm piece fresh ginger, peeled and finely chopped
4 garlic cloves, finely chopped
1–2 large green chillies, deseeded and finely chopped
4 large ripe tomatoes, chopped into dice
800 ml tinned coconut milk
zest and juice of 1 lemon
1 tbsp soft dark brown sugar
400 g sea bass fillet, skinned and thickly sliced
12 king prawns, peeled
100 g squid rings
12 fresh mussels, scrubbed and debearded (discard any with broken shells or that do not close when tapped on a work surface)
salt and freshly ground black pepper

- FOR THE GARNISH

handful of coriander leaves, roughly chopped
4 lemon wedges

Toast the coriander and cumin seeds in a dry frying pan until aromatic. Remove from the heat, stir in the cinnamon, mixed spice and set aside. Pour into a mortar and add a large pinch of salt. Grind the spices to a fine powder using a pestle.

Heat the vegetable oil in a frying pan over a medium heat, and fry the onion until soft and golden. Stir in the ginger, garlic, chilli and ground spices, and fry for a further 1 minute.

Add the tomatoes to the pan and cook for 5 minutes, or until softened.

Stir in the coconut milk, lemon zest and juice, and sugar, and bring to a simmer. Taste and season with salt and pepper.

Add the sea bass, prawns, squid and mussels to the pan, and gently poach in the coconut sauce for 5 minutes, or until just cooked through. The mussels should be wide open. Discard any that remain closed.

Divide the fish and shellfish among 4 shallow bowls, and ladle over the coconut sauce. Serve with steamed basmati rice garnished with coriander and lemon wedges.

# COURGETTE & ASPARAGUS RISOTTO WITH PINE NUTS, BASIL, MINT & LEMON

• SERVES 6

6 tbsp extra virgin olive oil
450 g medium courgettes, thinly sliced
400 g fresh asparagus spears, tough stalks removed, cut into 2.5 cm lengths
1 medium onion, finely chopped
2 garlic cloves, finely chopped
1.2 litres chicken or vegetable stock
400 g risotto rice (Arborio or Carnaroli)
zest and juice of 1 lemon
1 tbsp finely sliced mint
1 tbsp finely sliced basil
50 g pine nuts, toasted
salt and freshly ground black pepper
finely grated Parmesan, to serve

**When testing this recipe, my sons agreed that courgette is actually very good! The secret is to sauté the vegetables until al dente, and no further, to retain their bright green colour and bite.**

Heat the olive oil in a large frying pan and quickly sauté the courgettes, seasoned with salt and pepper, until just tender. Transfer to a bowl with a slotted spoon.

If needed, add another 1–2 tablespoons of olive oil to the pan, and sauté the asparagus until just tender. Add to the sautéed courgette and set aside.

Put the onion in the same pan, season with salt and pepper, and gently fry until it is soft but not coloured. Add the chopped garlic and fry for a further 30 seconds.

Meanwhile, heat the stock to a simmer in a separate, large pan and turn the heat to low.

Stir the rice into the onion mixture over a low heat until all the grains are coated and the rice becomes shiny and translucent.

Start to add the simmering stock, a ladleful at a time. Allow each ladle of stock to be absorbed before adding the next. Once all the stock has been added (this will take 20–30 minutes), test the rice. It should be tender with bite.

Stir in the lemon zest and juice, followed by the mint, basil and pine nuts. Taste and adjust the seasoning, if needed, then stir the sautéed courgette and asparagus into the rice.

To serve, spoon into warm bowls and serve with freshly grated Parmesan.

# CHINESE CHICKEN, MUSHROOM & GINGER HOTPOT

- SERVES 4–6

2 tbsp vegetable oil
1 tbsp toasted sesame oil
1.2 kg chicken thigh fillets, cut into 3 lengthways
125 g shiitake mushroom, halved lengthways
125 g oyster mushrooms halved lengthways
1 large onion, sliced
1 tsp Szechuan peppercorns
1 tbsp cornflour
1 litre rich chicken stock
2 tbsp rice wine vinegar
2 tbsp tamari
30 g fresh root ginger, peeled and thinly sliced
200 g baby corn
3 spring onions, sliced on the diagonal
large handful of beansprouts

**Tender chicken in a light and warming ginger and mushroom broth. Serve simply with fluffy jasmine rice or rice noodles and stir-fried greens.**

Heat the vegetable and sesame oils in a large pan. Season the chicken with salt and pepper, and lightly brown the chicken on all sides. Transfer the chicken to a bowl with a slotted spoon. Set aside.

Add the mushrooms and onion to the same pan, and fry gently until lightly browned. Add the Szechuan peppercorns, and fry for a further 30 seconds.

Stir the cornflour into the mushroom mixture. Gradually stir in the chicken stock, rice wine vinegar and tamari.

Return the chicken to the pan with the ginger, and bring the hotpot to a simmer. Cover with a lid and simmer for 1 hour or until the chicken is tender, regularly skimming off any fat rising to the surface.

Add the baby corn to the pan and cook for a further 15 minutes.

Stir the spring onions and beansprouts into the hotpot, then spoon the chicken and vegetables into warm, shallow bowls and ladle over the ginger broth. Serve with plain boiled rice and greens.

# FRENCH BRAISED LAMB WITH GARLIC, HERBS & HARICOT BEANS

**A traditional French stew that reminds me of happy long lunches in Paris with my family. Serve with mashed potatoes or brown rice, steamed green vegetables or a crisp green salad.**

- SERVES 4

2 tbsp extra virgin olive oil
900 g lamb neck fillet or boned shoulder of lamb, cut into pieces 5 x 2 cm
2 large onions, thinly sliced
1 bay leaf
3 thyme sprigs
2 rosemary sprigs
1 tbsp rice flour
200 ml lamb or chicken stock
200 ml white wine
10 unpeeled, whole garlic cloves
3 flat-leaf parsley sprigs
400 g tinned haricot beans, drained
½ tbsp lemon juice
salt and freshly ground black pepper
1 tbsp chopped flat-leaf parsley, to serve

Preheat the oven to 170°C.

Heat 2 tablespoons oil in a large flameproof casserole, over a medium heat, and add a handful of the diced lamb to the pan. Season with salt and pepper, and fry until the lamb is russet brown on all sides. Transfer the browned lamb to a bowl with a slotted spoon, and brown the remaining meat in batches in the same way, adding more oil, a tablespoon at a time, as needed.

Transfer all the browned meat to the bowl, then put the onion with the bay leaves, thyme and rosemary in the casserole. Season the vegetables with salt and pepper, and stir around to lift off browned bits stuck to the pan. Cover with the lid and cook over a very low heat for 20 minutes, or until the onions are soft and sweet, and have absorbed all the browned cooking juices. Remove the lid and stir in the rice flour, followed by the chicken stock and wine. Return the lamb to the casserole and add the garlic cloves, parsley and water to cover the lamb if needed. Bring the casserole to simmer, skimming any fat from the surface as it appears, then cover with the lid and cook in the oven for 1½ hours.

Skim off any fat on the surface of the casserole, and stir in the haricot beans. Continue to cook for a further 30 minutes, or until the lamb is sufficiently tender to be cut with a fork.

The sauce should be rich and syrupy. Stir in the lemon juice, taste and add more salt and pepper if needed. Lift out the sprigs of herbs and bay leaves.

To serve, sprinkle with chopped parsley. Ask your guests to squeeze the soft garlic out of the skins to fully enjoy the flavours of the dish.

*Tip*

**Cooking the garlic cloves in their skins softens and sweetens their flavour, perfectly complementing the tender sweet lamb and beans.**

# SMOKY LAMB, TOMATO & BEAN STEW

**A warming winter stew with gentle smoky spiciness. Use stewing beef or chicken thighs as an alternative to lamb. Chipotle peppers are available in the speciality sections of most large supermarkets.**

In a small bowl, pour boiling water over the chipotle chillies and leave to soak for 30 minutes.

Heat the oil in a medium pan over a medium heat, then season the lamb with salt and pepper. Brown the meat in batches, being careful not to overcrowd the pan and lifting out with a slotted to rest on warm plate.

Once all the meat has been browned, fry the onion and pepper until golden brown. Stir in the garlic, spices, cinnamon stick and herbs and fry for a further 30 seconds.

Drain the soaked chipotle chillies, chop finely and add to the pan with the chicken stock, tomatoes and fresh coriander. Stir in the browned lamb (any any juices) and bring to the simmer.

Simmer for 1¼ hours, skimming any fat and scum from the surface every 30 minutes. Stir in the haricot and kidney beans, then cook for a further 20 minutes, or until the meat is very tender. Check the seasoning.

Serve with brown rice, steamed green vegetables and soured cream.

- SERVES 4–6

1½ dried chipotle chillies
2 tbsp vegetable oil
1.2 kg boned lamb shoulder, trimmed of fat and cut into pieces 5 x 2 cm
1 large onion, thinly sliced
2 red peppers, deseeded and thinly sliced
1 yellow pepper, deseeded and thinly sliced
4 garlic cloves, finely chopped
2 tsp ground coriander
2 tsp ground cumin
3 tsp smoked paprika
1 cinnamon stick
2 tsp mixed dried herbs
500 ml rich chicken stock
800 g tinned chopped tomatoes
6 coriander stalks
400 g tinned haricot beans
400 g tinned red kidney beans
salt and freshly ground black pepper

- TO SERVE

roughly chopped fresh coriander
soured cream

# BEEF, ROOT VEGETABLE & RED WINE STEW WITH SOFT POLENTA

- SERVES 4

4 tbsp vegetable oil or light olive oil
700g braising or stewing steak such as chuck steak, trimmed of fat and cut into pieces 5 x 2 cm
3 medium onions, thinly sliced
3 medium carrots, cut into 2-cm cubes
2 parsnips, cut into 2-cm cubes
1 tbsp rice flour
290 ml red wine
290 ml chicken or beef stock
2 bay leaves
2 thyme sprigs
3 medium waxy potatoes, peeled and cut into cubes
salt and freshly ground black pepper

- FOR THE SOFT POLENTA

750 ml chicken stock
200 g instant polenta
60 g Parmesan, finely grated
40 g butter, diced

*Tip*

**For something different, add pan-fried bacon lardons and mushrooms to the stew or make a pie by topping the cooked stew with a puff or shortcrust pastry lid. For instructions, see page 123.**

**A hearty family stew made all the more comforting when served with soft polenta, rice or quinoa.**

Preheat the oven to 150°C.

Heat the oil in a large flameproof casserole over a medium heat, and fry a handful of seasoned and prepared beef at a time, to a rich brown colour. Transfer the browned meat to a bowl. Set aside.

Add the onions, carrots and parsnips to the casserole, season with salt and pepper, and gently fry, stirring regularly, until browned on all sides. Stir in 1 the rice flour, followed by the wine and stock. Scrape the browned juices from the bottom and sides of the pan with a wooden spoon.

Return the browned meat to the casserole and add the bay leaves and thyme. If needed, add more water to the pan to cover all the ingredients, and bring to a simmer, spooning off any fat that rises to the surface.

Cover the casserole with a tight-fitting lid and cook in the middle of the oven for 1½ hours, skimming off any fat from time to time.

Add the potatoes and cook the casserole for a further 30 minutes, or until the meat is sufficiently tender to be cut with a fork.

Meanwhile, make the polenta by bringing the chicken stock to the boil in a large pan. Pour the polenta into the stock in a thin, steady stream, whisking continuously. Continue to whisk the mixture for 4–5 minutes while the polenta simmers and thickens. It is ready when the stock has been fully absorbed and the thickened polenta falls cleanly away from the sides of the pan.

Stir in the Parmesan and butter, season with salt and pepper and cover to keep warm while you finish the stew.

Remove the casserole from the oven and skim off any remaining fat. The sauce should be richly coloured and thick enough to coat the back of a spoon. If the sauce is too thin, strain the liquid into a clean pan and reduce by fast-boiling to the desired consistency. Return the thickened liquid to the casserole. Taste and season again if needed.

Spoon the stew over mounds of polenta, and serve immediately.

# PARMESAN & ROSEMARY POLENTA CHIPS

**These crispy, flavoursome chips are a delicious alternative to potato chips and go particularly well with rich stews and braised dishes, as well as salads and fish.**

- SERVES 4–6

light olive oil, for greasing
750 ml vegetable or chicken stock
200 g instant polenta
50 g Parmesan, finely grated
1 tbsp extra virgin olive oil, plus 2 tbsp extra for drizzling
1 tbsp finely chopped fresh rosemary
salt and freshly ground black pepper

Lightly grease a shallow 22 x 30cm baking sheet with light olive oil.

Bring the stock to the boil in a large pan. Pour the polenta in a thin, steady stream into the boiling stock, stirring continuously for 4–5 minutes until the polenta has thickened and all the stock has been absorbed. Remove from the heat and stir in the Parmesan, 1 tablespoon of olive oil, half the rosemary and a few grinds of pepper.

Pour the polenta over the bottom of the baking sheet, and spread out evenly using the back of a spoon. Cover with non-stick baking paper and set aside to cool. Place in the fridge for 4 hours or overnight to set.

About 30 minutes before you want to start cooking the chips, preheat the oven to 200°C.

Turn the polenta out onto a chopping board and, with a sharp knife, cut into even, finger-sized chips.

Arrange the chips in a single layer over the bottom of a large roasting tin and drizzle with the remaining olive oil. Mix the remaining rosemary with a large pinch of salt, and sprinkle over the chips. Bake in the oven for 30 minutes until the chips are crisp and golden, turning them over halfway through cooking. Serve immediately.

- VARIATION: GRILLED POLENTA

Prepare the polenta and leave to set, then cut into slices 2 cm thick. Brush with olive oil and grill in a dry frying pan or on a griddle. Sprinkle with chopped rosemary and salt, and serve.

# TUNA BAKED WITH VINE CHERRY TOMATOES & NEW POTATOES, CAPERS, BLACK OLIVES, ROSEMARY & LEMON

- SERVES 4

4 x 120-g tuna steaks, each 2 cm thick
2 tbsp extra virgin olive oil
salt and black pepper

- FOR THE POTATOES

800 g new potatoes, halved lengthways
1 lemon, cut into 6 wedges
1 tbsp capers, rinsed and drained
80 g black olives, pitted and halved
4 garlic cloves, finely chopped
1 tbsp chopped rosemary
12–16 ripe cherry tomatoes on the vine, cut into groups of 3 or 4 tomatoes
2 tbsp extra virgin olive oil
salt and freshly ground black pepper

**This dish, full of summer flavour and colour, is an easy yet impressive dish to enjoy with friends. Serve with a lightly dressed green salad.**

Preheat the oven to 180°C.

Spread the potato halves over the bottom of a large roasting tin. Squeeze the juice from each lemon wedge over the potatoes, then tuck wedges among the potatoes. The oils in the peel will enhance the lemony flavour.

Mix together the capers, black olives, garlic and rosemary, and sprinkle over the potatoes.

Arrange the vine cherry tomatoes on top of the potatoes, drizzle the oil over the vegetables, then season lightly with salt and generously with pepper. Bake in the oven for 45 minutes, or until the potatoes are crisp and golden.

Meanwhile, heat a large frying pan or griddle over a high heat. Brush the tuna steaks on both sides with the olive oil, and season with salt and pepper. Place the tuna steaks in the hot pan, and sear for 1–2 minutes on each side, or until the steaks are browned on the outside but remain rare in the centre.

To serve, remove the lemon wedges from the potatoes and spoon the potatoes onto warm plates. Place a tuna steak on top with 3 or 4 cherry tomatoes on the vine. Serve immediately.

*Tip*

**Try replacing the tuna steaks with pan-fried salmon fillets, a small sea bass per person or seasoned chicken breasts.**

# PAN-FRIED PORK CHOPS WITH CIDER SAUCE, SAUTÉED APPLES & CHAMP

**Normandy meets Ireland in this attractive and flavoursome dish. The tender sweetness of the sautéed apple goes beautifully with the pork and the spring onion mash, otherwise known as champ.**

- SERVES 4

1 tbsp vegetable oil
4 thickly cut pork chops on the bone
2 tsp rice flour
200 ml medium cider
200 ml chicken stock
2 thyme sprigs
3 Granny Smith apples, peeled, cored and cut into 8 wedges
30 g butter or 1 tbsp extra virgin olive oil

- FOR THE CHAMP

200 ml whole milk or dairy-free milk
30 g butter or 1½ tbsp extra virgin olive oil
3 spring onions, thinly sliced on the diagonal
750 g floury potatoes such as Maris Piper or King Edward, peeled and quartered
salt and freshly ground black pepper

Preheat the oven to 60°C.

To prepare the champ, pour the milk into a small pan, then add the butter and spring onions, and season with salt and pepper. Heat the milk to simmering point, then turn off the heat. Leave the milk to cool, to infuse with the flavour of spring onions.

In a medium pan, cover the potatoes with water, season with salt and simmer for 15–20 minutes until the potatoes are tender when tested with a table knife. Drain and leave to steam dry for 2 minutes.

Meanwhile, to prepare the pork, heat the oil in a large frying pan over a medium heat. Lightly season the pork chops with salt and pepper, and pan-fry for 5–6 minutes on each side until the fat is golden and crisp, and the meat is browned and cooked through. Transfer the pork chops to an ovenproof dish and keep warm in the oven.

Tip all but 1 tablespoon of the fat out of the pan. Off the heat, stir the rice flour into the fat, then gradually stir in the cider and chicken stock to form a smooth sauce. Return the pan to the heat, add the thyme sprigs and stir until the sauce thickens to a syrupy consistency, then simmer for 1 minute. Taste and season if needed. Discard the thyme, then pour the sauce around the pork chops and return the dish to the warming oven.

To prepare the apples, heat the butter in the frying pan until the foam subsides (or use oil), then tip in the apple wedges. Season with salt and pepper and sauté until golden brown on all sides. Scatter the apples over the pork and return to the oven while you finish the champ.

Return the flavoured milk to the heat and bring to a simmer. Tip the potatoes from the colander into a medium pan and pour in the milk. Mash until smooth. Season with more salt and pepper if needed.

Spoon the champ onto warm plates, then top with a pork chop. Next, spoon over the apples and sauce, and serve immediately.

**This is also good made with gluten-free sausages, chicken breasts or loin of cod or haddock in place of the pork.**

# SPANISH CHICKEN WITH PEPPERS, GARLIC, OLIVES & ROSEMARY SERVED WITH CELERIAC, POTATO & OLIVE OIL MASH

- SERVES 4

2 tbsp extra virgin olive oil
4 chicken drumsticks and 4 chicken thighs
4 rosemary sprigs
2 medium red onions, quartered
2 medium red peppers, deseeded and cut lengthways into 8 slices
100 ml oloroso sherry
3 tbsp sherry vinegar
250 ml chicken stock
8 unpeeled garlic cloves,
150 g black olives

- FOR THE CELERIAC, POTATO AND OLIVE OIL MASH

250 g floury potatoes such as Maris Piper or King Edward, peeled and cut into 2-cm cubes
500 g celeriac, peeled and cut into 2-cm cubes
2 tbsp extra virgin olive oil
150 ml whole milk or dairy-free milk
salt and freshly ground black pepper

**This recipe looks and smells as good as it tastes. It is regularly requested by my boys for supper at the weekend, which suits me because it is full of goodness and quick to prepare. The vibrant flavours of the roasted vegetables and Spanish sherry sauce pair beautifully with the gutsy celeriac and potato mash.**

Preheat the oven to 180°C.

Heat the olive oil in a frying pan over a medium heat, season the chicken pieces with salt and pepper, and fry until golden brown on all sides. Place in a single layer in a large roasting dish, and tuck the rosemary sprigs underneath. Brown the onion and pepper in the oil in the pan, then arrange around the chicken in the roasting dish.

Pour the sherry, vinegar and stock into the same pan, and bring to the boil, scraping up the browned juices from the base and sides of the pan with a wooden spoon. Simmer for 2 minutes, then pour over the chicken. Scatter over the whole garlic cloves and olives, and press them into the sauce. Add a little water if needed to cover the garlic cloves, to ensure they do not burn during baking.

Cover the roasting dish with foil and roast for 30 minutes. Remove the foil and roast for another 30 minutes until the chicken is beginning to fall away from the bone. Tip the pan to the side and skim off any excess oil and fat collected on the surface of the sauce.

While the chicken is cooking, prepare the celeriac and potato mash. Place the potato and celeriac in a large pan, cover with cold water and season with a large pinch of salt. Bring to the boil and simmer for 10–15 minutes until the celeriac and potato are tender when tested with a table knife. Drain in a colander and leave the potatoes and celeriac to steam dry for 2 minutes. Return to the pan, season with salt and pepper and mash to a smooth purée with the olive oil and milk.

Heap the mash onto warm plates, top with chicken and vegetables, and spoon over the sauce. Serve immediately, asking your guests to squeeze the soft garlic out of the skins onto the chicken and vegetables.

# ROOT VEGETABLE GRATIN

- SERVES 6

500 ml double cream
1 heaped tsp Dijon mustard
50 g butter
600 g floury potatoes, peeled and thinly sliced
1 medium onion, thinly sliced
200 g celeriac, peeled and thinly sliced
200 g parsnips, thinly sliced
100 g Gruyère cheese, grated
salt and freshly ground black pepper

**Potato gratin is the ultimate comfort dish at the best of times. Replacing a proportion of the potato with celeriac and parsnip makes a really tasty change. Serve this dish with Pork Escalopes with Lemon, Garlic and Rosemary (page 93), roast and cold meats and chicken.**

Preheat the oven to 180°C.

Whisk the cream and mustard together.

Butter a 1-litre ovenproof dish and spread out half the potato slices over the bottom, followed by half of the onion, celeriac and parsnip. Season with salt and pepper.

Pour over half of the mustard and cream mixture and sprinkle over half of the Gruyère cheese. Repeat the layering again with the remaining ingredients, and sprinkle over the remaining Gruyère.

Place the dish in a roasting tray and bake in the oven for 45–60 minutes until the potatoes, parsnip and celeriac are tender when tested with a sharp knife and the top is golden and crisp.

Cut into 6 portions and serve immediately.

# ROAST GAMMON WITH ROAST MAPLE-GLAZED ROOT VEGETABLES

**A perfect roast for autumnal and wintry weekends. The rich but subtle sweetness of the roasted vegetables perfectly accompanies the saltiness of gammon, but also goes beautifully with other roast meats, poultry, game, sausages and cooked cold meats.**

- SERVES 4

2 kg smoked gammon with the rind scored

- FOR THE MAPLE-GLAZED ROOT VEGETABLES

2 medium floury potatoes, peeled and cut into 6 wedges
2 medium parsnips, cut into quarters lengthways
8 baby carrots or 4 medium carrots, cut in half, lengthways
2 medium leeks, cut into 4 pieces
4 baby turnips, trimmed at the root and shoot
2 medium beetroot, scrubbed, root and shoot removed cut into 4 wedges
4 large garlic cloves, unpeeled
4 rosemary sprigs
1 tbsp light olive oil
2 tbsp maple syrup
salt and freshly ground black pepper

Preheat the oven to 200°C.

Roast the gammon, tied with string or in netting, in a large roasting tin in the oven for 20 minutes per 500 g.

About 1 hour before the gammon is to finish cooking, scatter the prepared root vegetables around the gammon in the tin, then turn them over in the gammon fat, adding the 1 tablespoon of oil if needed. Tuck the whole garlic cloves and rosemary sprigs between the vegetables, and season lightly with salt and pepper.

Roast in the oven for 45 minutes, or until the vegetables are tender and turning golden brown. Remove the tin from the oven, and stir the maple syrup into the vegetables. Return to the oven and roast for a further 5–10 minutes.

Insert a skewer into the centre of the gammon to check it is cooked. When pulled out, the skewer should be piping hot. The crackling should also be brittle and dark golden brown. If the gammon requires further cooking, transfer the joint to another roasting dish and return to the oven. With a slotted spoon, transfer the vegetables to a serving dish and cover with foil to keep warm.

To make the sauce, tip the roasting pan so that the cooking juices collect in one corner, and spoon off any fat, being careful to retain the dark cooking juices. Add 100 ml water to the pan and loosen the browned juices from the bottom of the pan with a wooden spoon over a low heat. Once the gammon is cooked, remove the string or netting holding the crackling in place, then use a carving knife to cut the crackling away from the gammon; snap into 8 pieces.

To serve, spoon the maple-glazed vegetables onto warm plates and, top with thinly sliced gammon, 1–2 spoons of the rich maple sauce and shards of crackling.

# PASTRY

**The fact that gluten-free pastry does not contain gluten is both helpful and unhelpful. When making gluten-rich pastry, the aim is to knead and roll it as little as possible, in order to minimise the development of the elastic gluten in the flour, which can cause the pastry to shrink and become tough.**

There is no such problem with gluten-free pastry, and so, provided the pastry stays cool, it can be rolled out and reworked a number of times, without affecting the quality of the cooked pastry. Gluten in wheat flour firmly binds pastry dough together as it is rolled out, shaped and baked. It also helps to hold baked shortcrust pastry together and contributes to its crisp texture. By contrast, gluten-free pastry is bound only by the fat and egg, and as a result is more delicate to handle during rolling and shaping when raw, and more likely to crumble when baked. The good news is that gluten-free pastry, when made with the correct proportions of flour, fat and egg and rolled with the support of cling film or greaseproof paper, is a joy to work with and tastes lighter, if not better than its gluten-rich equivalent. Here are some tips to help you make great shortcrust pastry.

## BINDING PASTRY DOUGH TOGETHER

To bind gluten-free pastry, use only whole beaten egg because this binds the raw dough and baked pastry more strongly than water or a mixture of egg and water. Gluten-free dry ingredients take longer to absorb liquid than wheat flour, which can make the pastry dough crumbly to handle. Mix the pastry dough together until it comes together in large lumps. Knead the dough until it forms a smooth ball, and leave to stand for 5–10 minutes before rolling and shaping.

## ROLLING OUT SHORTCRUST PASTRY

Roll gluten-free pastry dough to the required thickness between 2 large sheets of cling film or greaseproof paper, to help hold it together.

The cling film and greaseproof paper also help to support the pastry as it is used to line tart tins and prepare pie crusts.

With the rolling pin, press and flatten the ball of pastry into a rough circle, about 2.5 cm thick.

With firm strokes, roll out the pastry into a large circle to the required thickness, turning the pastry a quarter turn every 4 rolls, to ensure that it is rolled evenly.

## LINING A TIN WITH SHORTCRUST PASTRY

To line a 20-cm tart tin you will need a quantity of shortcrust pastry made with 220 g flour and 110 g fat.

### TO LINE THE TIN

- Roll out the pastry to 3 mm thick, then peel off the top sheet of cling film.
- Place the pastry into the tin with the side covered in cling film uppermost.
- Gently press the pastry in the tin, so that the pastry hugs the bottom, corners and sides of the tin.
- Bend the extra pastry standing above the rim outwards, then roll a rolling pin over the rim of the tin to trim the edge.
- Carefully peel away the second layer of cling film.
- Use the trimmings to patch up any holes and cracks that may have appeared while lining the tin.
- If the pastry is feeling very soft, place the tart shell in the fridge for 30 minutes to firm up before baking. Cold, firm pastry is less likely to lose its shape when cooking in the oven.

## BLIND BAKING

To ensure the pastry case remains crisp after the tart is filled and baked, it is first blind-baked until crisp and golden brown. Blind baking involves lining the raw pastry tart shell with foil or greaseproof paper and weighing it down with a thin layer of baking beans, rice or dried lentils, which help to maintain the shape of the empty tart shell as it cooks.

#### TO BLIND-BAKE A PASTRY TART SHELL

Preheat the oven to 200°C.

Cut out a large circle of greaseproof paper and crumple it into a ball (to soften it so that it fits tightly into the corners of the pastry case). Open out the paper and use it to line the pastry before weighing it down with 2–3 tablespoons of baking beans, lentils or rice.

Bake the lined pastry case for 15 minutes, or until the pastry is dry and firm. Remove the greaseproof paper and beans, and continue to bake for another 5–10 minutes until the pastry base is evenly cooked and light golden.

Leave the pastry in the tin to cool on a wire rack before adding any filling to the pastry case.

## ASSEMBLING A PIE WITH SHORTCRUST PASTRY

To line a pie dish for a double-crust pie, use the method described for lining a tart tin and blind-bake as described.

- For a single-crust pie, consisting of a filling covered with a shortcrust or puff pastry lid, place the filling in the pie dish.
- Peel the top sheet of cling film off pastry rolled to between 3 mm and 5 mm thick and 5 cm larger than the pie dish on all sides.
- Trim a narrow strip of pastry off all sides.
- Wet the pie dish rim with beaten egg or water, and press the pastry strips on to the rim of the dish.
- Place the pastry lid, pastry side down, over the filling.
- Press the edges of the pastry lid onto the pastry-covered rim of the pie, then remove the second sheet of cling film. Trim away any excess pastry outside the dish with a sharp knife. This forms a firm base to attach the pie lid.
- Crimp the edge with your fingers or using a fork.
- Make a small hole in the centre of the pastry lid, to allow steam to escape.

#### FOR SAVOURY PIES

Brush the pastry lid with beaten egg mixed with a pinch of salt, decorate with shaped pastry trimmings and glaze with beaten egg again.

#### FOR SWEET PIES

Brush the pastry lid with beaten egg mixed with a large pinch of sugar. Decorate with shaped pastry trimmings, glaze with egg again and sprinkle with granulated or demerara sugar.

## ROLLING OUT PUFF PASTRY

Gluten-free puff pastry is very difficult to make at home due to the delicate nature of the dough and the accuracy necessary to create uniform layers of fat through it. These all-important fat layers trap air, which expand as the pastry is baked, causing each layer to puff, rise and set.

To make the most of these fat layers, it is important not to break them. The fat layers run at right angles through the pastry, so always keep the rectangular shape of puff pastry, rolling at right angles, and cut the required shape out of the rectangle with sharp knife.

#### FOR TART BASES

Roll out puff pastry to 3 mm thick and prick all over with a fork, leaving a 2-cm border around the edge. This way the base will stay flat and edges will rise to form a rim.

#### FOR PIE LIDS

Roll between 3 mm and 5 mm thick.

# BUTTERNUT SQUASH, FETA, SAGE & PINE NUT TART

**This is a very colourful and tasty tart to quickly prepare for an impromptu light meal with friends. Serve with salad and new potatoes.**

- SERVES 6

750 g butternut squash, peeled, deseeded and cut into 1.5-cm cubes
2 tbsp extra virgin olive oil
1 tbsp thyme leaves
12 pitted kalamata olives, halved lengthways
2 tbsp pine nuts
100 g feta, crumbled
1 x 400 g block gluten-free puff pastry, defrosted
240 g fresh ricotta
2 garlic cloves, finely chopped
1 tbsp chopped sage
salt and freshly ground black pepper

Preheat the oven to 200°C. Place cubes of butternut squash on a baking tray and drizzle with the olive oil. Season with salt and pepper, sprinkle over half the thyme, and toss to combine. Roast in the oven for 30 minutes, or until the squash is tender but not browned. Remove from the oven and set aside to cool. Increase the oven temperature to 220°C.

When the butternut squash is cool, mix with the olives, pine nuts and feta.

Roll out the puff pastry into a rectangle 25 cm x 30 cm and 3 mm thick. Place on a baking sheet and prick all over with a fork, leaving a 2-cm border around the edge of the pastry.

Mix the ricotta, garlic cloves, remaining thyme and sage together in a small bowl. Season with salt and pepper. Spread over the pastry. Top with the butternut mixture, and bake for 30–40 minutes until the pastry is risen and golden. Serve cut into squares.

# CREAMY SMOKED HADDOCK, PARMESAN & PARSLEY TART

- SERVES 6

300 g smoked haddock
about 500 ml whole milk
2 bay leaves
1 large onion, finely chopped
30 g butter
30 g cornflour
150 ml double cream
½ tsp freshly ground nutmeg
20 g Parmesan cheese, finely grated, plus 1 tbsp extra, to garnish
2 eggs, beaten
1 tbsp finely chopped flat-leaf parsley
squeeze of lemon juice
salt and freshly ground black pepper

- FOR THE PASTRY

110 g fine cornmeal
110 g rice flour
110 g cold butter, diced
30 g Parmesan cheese, finely grated
1 medium egg, beaten
salt and freshly ground black pepper

**A rich and creamy tart, perfect served with a baby spinach leaf, tomato and spring onion salad. Use this crisp and cheesy pastry for other savoury tarts too.**

Preheat the oven to 180°C.

To make the pastry, sift the cornmeal, rice flour, a pinch of salt and 3 grinds of pepper into a bowl. Rub the butter into the flour with your fingertips (or pulse in a processor) until the mixture resembles fine breadcrumbs. Stir (or pulse) in the Parmesan, followed by the beaten egg, until the pastry comes together. Gently knead the pastry until it forms a smooth ball.

Roll out and use to line a 24-cm wide tart tin. Blind-bake the tart shell, following the instructions on page 123.

Meanwhile, arrange the smoked haddock, skin-side down, in a frying pan. Cover the fish with milk, add the bay leaves, season with pepper and bring to a gentle simmer over a medium heat. Turn down the heat, and simmer the fish for 10 minutes, or until the fish separates into tender flakes when gently pressed. Remove from the heat and pour the poaching milk into a measuring jug.

Flake the fish, removing any skin and bones, and place in a bowl to cool.

In a medium pan, gently fry the onion in the butter until soft but not coloured. Stir in the cornflour and cook for 1 minute. Remove the pan from the heat and slowly stir in the 300 ml of poaching milk (with the bay leaves), cream and nutmeg.

Return the pan to the heat, and slowly bring the onion mixture to the boil, stirring continuously. Simmer for 1 minute, then remove from the heat. Remove the bay leaves and stir in the 20 g Parmesan cheese. Beat in the eggs, and gently stir in the flaked fish, parsley and lemon juice. Season as needed with salt, pepper and more lemon juice.

Pour the mixture into the pastry case, sprinkle with the extra Parmesan cheese and bake in the centre of the oven for 30–40 minutes until the centre of the filling is set and the tart is light golden brown.

Serve in generous slices, hot or cold, with salad and new potatoes.

# ROAST TOMATO, BASIL PESTO & BLACK OLIVE TART

**This is a quick to prepare but impressive tart for a light meal. Serve with Warm Puy Lentil, Goat's Cheese, Smoked Bacon and Baby Spinach Salad (page 74) to transport you and your guests to Provence.**

- SERVES 6

- FOR THE PASTRY

55 g buckwheat flour
110 g rice flour, plus extra for dusting
55 g cornflour
large pinch of salt
110 g cold butter or dairy-free hard baking margarine
1 egg, beaten
rice flour, for dusting

- FOR THE TART FILLING

2 heaped tbsp of basil and pinenut pesto
4 large ripe vine tomatoes, thickly sliced into rounds
handful of fresh basil leaves, shredded
125 g yellow and red cherry tomatoes, halved
handful of provençal or kalamata olives
1 tbsp extra virgin olive oil
2 garlic cloves, thinly sliced
salt and freshly ground black pepper
basil leaves, to garnish

Preheat the oven to 200°C.

To make the pastry, sift the flours and salt into a bowl. Rub the fat into the flour with your fingertips (or pulse in a processor) until the mixture resembles breadcrumbs. Stir (or pulse) in the beaten egg, until the pastry comes together. Knead the pastry until it forms a smooth ball.

Roll out and use to line a 24 cm wide tart tin. Blind-bake the tart shell, following the instructions on page 123.

Spread the pesto evenly over the baked pastry base, then layer the sliced vine tomatoes in overlapping circles on the basil pesto, seasoning each layer with salt and pepper, and a sprinkling of shredded basil.

Scatter the cherry tomatoes and black olives over the tomato slices.

Gently heat the oil with the sliced garlic until the garlic starts to sizzle, then drizzle over the tart. Season with salt and pepper, scatter on some basil leaves and bake in the oven for 30 minutes, or until the tomatoes are soft and slightly browning around the edges.

Serve either warm or cold, scattered with freshly torn basil leaves.

# CHICKEN, LEEK & TARRAGON PIE

- SERVES 4–6

800 g chicken thigh fillets
½ onion, sliced
2 tarragon sprigs
2 bay leaves
800 ml chicken stock
30 g butter or 1 tbsp vegetable oil
3 medium leeks, thickly sliced
1 heaped tbsp cornflour
1 tbsp chopped tarragon leaves
salt and freshly ground black pepper

- FOR THE PASTRY LID

1 x 400-g pack gluten-free puff pastry or 2 quantities Buckwheat Shortcrust Pastry (page 127)
1 egg, beaten, to glaze

**This warming and aromatic pie is simple and quick to make with a defrosted pack of gluten-free puff pastry. Alternatively make the pie lid with buckwheat shortcrust pastry, used for the Roast Tomato, Basil Pesto and Black Olive Tart (page 127). Delicious served with buttery mashed potato and steamed green beans.**

Preheat the oven to 200°C.

Place the chicken, onion, tarragon sprigs and bay leaves in a medium pan. Pour over the chicken stock and additional water to cover. Season with salt and pepper, and bring to the boil. Turn down the heat and simmer for 30 minutes. Strain the stock into a bowl, and discard the herbs. Set aside. Cut each chicken thigh into 3, lengthways and tip into a 1.5-litre ovenproof pie dish with a rim at least 1 cm thick.

In a separate pan, melt the butter (or heat the oil) and gently fry the leeks, seasoned with salt and pepper and cover with a lid, until soft. Stir the cornflour into the leeks off the heat, then gradually stir in the reserved chicken stock. Return the pan to the heat, and stir the sauce until it comes to the boil and thickens to coating consistency. Stir in the chopped tarragon and check the seasoning. Pour the sauce over the chicken, and gently stir to ensure the sauce and chicken are evenly mixed.

Roll out the pastry into a rectangle 3 mm thick and slightly larger than the pie dish. Cut strips of pastry along the edges of the pastry rectangle, press onto the rim of the pie dish and brush with beaten egg. Cover the chicken filling with the trimmed rectangle of pastry. Gently press the edges of the pastry lid onto the pastry-covered rim, then crimp with your fingers or with the tines of a fork to seal the pie. Brush the pie lid with a little more beaten egg, then place in the middle of the oven and bake for 45–60 minutes until the pie lid is crisp and golden brown.

To serve, first run a sharp knife between the rim of the pie dish and the pastry lid. Cut the pie into 4–6 portions, and lift the pastry and filling with a large spoon onto warm plates.

# GREEK SPINACH & FETA PIE

**This is a truly delicious vegetarian pie that even the keenest carnivore will enjoy. Serve as part of a buffet lunch or simply with salad for a light meal.**

Preheat the oven to 180°C.

To make the pastry, sift the flours, ground almonds and salt into a bowl. Rub the butter into the flour with your fingertips until the mixture resembles breadcrumbs. Stir in the beaten egg until the pastry comes together. Gently knead the pastry until it forms a smooth ball and divide in two. Set one aside for the lid.

Roll out the second portion of dough, and use to line a 24-cm wide tart tin. Blind-bake the tart base following the instructions on page 123. Remove the pie base from the oven and brush with a little of the beaten egg. Return to the oven for a further 2 minutes. This will help to keep the pie base crisp.

Meanwhile, in a large pan, gently fry the onions in the olive oil, seasoned with salt and pepper, over a low heat until soft but not coloured. This will take about 15 minutes. Add the spring onions and garlic to the pan, and fry for a further minute. Stir in the spinach, herbs and nutmeg. Cover with a lid and steam the spinach for 5 minutes, or until the leaves have wilted.

Pour the spinach mixture into a colander to drain, and leave to cool.

In a large bowl, mix the 2 beaten eggs with the feta and Parmesan. Stir in the cooled spinach, a small pinch of salt and 4 grinds of pepper.

Tip the mixture into the blind-baked pastry case, and flatten out with a spoon. Roll out the remaining pastry dough between sheets of clingfilm into a round 3 mm thick between sheets of cling film. Peel off the top layer of cling film and lay the pastry over the spinach filling. Gently press the edge of the pastry lid onto the edge of the pastry base. Trim away the extra pastry around the edge with a sharp knife. Make a small hole in the centre of the pie to allow steam to escape, and decorate the pie with the pastry trimmings cut into leaves if you wish.

Glaze the pastry lid with a little beaten egg, and bake in the centre of the oven for 45–60 minutes until the pie is crisp and golden.

Leave the pie to cool for 10 minutes, then slice into generous portions with a sharp knife and serve.

- SERVES 4

3 medium onions, diced
2 tbsp extra virgin oil
1 bunch of spring onions, finely sliced
2 garlic cloves, finely chopped
500 g spinach leaves, washed, dried and roughly chopped
2 tbsp roughly chopped flat-leaf parsley
2 tbsp roughly chopped dill
½ tsp freshly grated nutmeg
400 g feta cheese, crumbled
2 tbsp freshly grated Parmesan
2 eggs, beaten
salt and freshly ground black pepper

- FOR THE PASTRY

110 g buckwheat flour
110 g rice flour
110 g cornflour
110 g ground almonds
large pinch of salt
220 g cold butter
1 egg, beaten, plus 1 extra, to glaze

# MOROCCAN SPICED LAMB SHANK, APRICOT & CHICKPEA PIE

- SERVES 4

1 x 400 g block gluten-free puff pastry, defrosted to room temperature
4 tbsp vegetable oil
4 lamb shanks
75 ml dry white wine
1 red pepper, deseeded and cut into thick slices lengthways
1 large onion, sliced thickly
3 garlic cloves, finely chopped
2-cm piece of fresh root ginger, peeled and finely chopped
1 tsp cumin seeds
2 tsp ground coriander
2 bay leaves
1 cinnamon stick
1 heaped tbsp cornflour
400 g tinned chopped tomatoes
300 ml chicken stock
pinch of saffron threads
85 g dried apricots, halved lengthways
400 g tinned chickpeas, drained
1 heaped tbsp kalamata olives
½ lemon, cut into 4 wedges
handful of mint leaves
1 egg beaten
salt and freshly ground black pepper

**An impressive-looking and fabulous-tasting pie to serve your hungry guests on a cold winter's day.**

Preheat the oven to 150°C.

To make the pie filling, in a medium casserole, first brown the lamb shanks, seasoned with salt and pepper, in half the oil. Transfer to a bowl. Pour the wine into the pan, and loosen browned bits with a wooden spoon. Boil for 30 seconds. Pour over the shanks.

Brown the peppers and onion in the remaining oil. Add the garlic, ginger, cumin, coriander, bay leaves and cinnamon to the pan and fry for a further 30 seconds. Stir in the cornflour, tomatoes, stock and saffron.

Arrange the lamb shanks among the vegetables in the pan, add water to cover and bring to a simmer, skimming off any fat that rises to the surface. Cover with a lid and braise in the oven for 2 hours, or until the meat is tender but not falling away from the bone. After 1½ hours spoon off any fat then stir in the apricots, chickpeas, and olives.

When the lamb shanks are cooked, arrange them in a 2-litre deep ovenproof pie dish with the bones pointing upwards. Strain the sauce into a clean pan, and scatter the chickpeas, olives, apricots and vegetables around the shanks.

Increase the oven temperature to 180°C.

Add the lemon wedges and mint to the sauce, and boil vigorously until the sauce is rich, syrupy and reduced to 750 ml. Discard the mint and lemon. Season with salt and pepper, and pour around the lamb shanks.

Roll out the pastry into a large rectangle 5 mm thick and slightly larger than the pie dish. Press a thin strip of pastry around the rim of the dish and brush with a little beaten egg. Gently press the pastry lid onto the pastry collar and crimp the edges with your fingers or with a fork. Brush the pie lid with beaten egg, and bake for 45–60 minutes until the pie lid is crisp and golden brown.

To serve, cut the pastry lid into quarters and transfer the lamb shanks topped with pastry to warm plates along with the vegetables and sauce.

# Puddings

To present a memorable and beautiful pudding is extremely satisfying. Using gluten-free pastry, you can make fruit tarts and pies, and for something sweet and moreish try my Sticky Date and Toffee Pudding or Self-saucing Rich Chocolate Mocha Pudding.

# SUMMER BERRY TART

- SERVES 4–6

- FOR THE RICE AND ALMOND PASTRY

110 g rice flour
55 g cornflour
55 g ground almonds
pinch of salt
110 g cold butter or dairy-free hard baking margarine, cut into small pieces
70 g caster sugar
1 egg, beaten

- FOR THE VANILLA CUSTARD FILLING

40 g cornflour
85 g caster sugar
290 ml milk or dairy-free soya or rice milk
1 vanilla pod, split lengthways
100 ml double cream or dairy-free soy cream

- FOR THE FRUIT

400 g medium fresh strawberries
110 g fresh raspberries
handful of fresh blueberries
1 tbsp icing sugar for dusting

- VARIATION

For a quick and easy alternative to vanilla custard, sweeten 290 ml of crème fraîche with 2 tablespoons of caster sugar, and use to fill the pastry shell in place of the vanilla custard.

Use this recipe to make individual summer berry tartlets for petit fours.

**A beautiful tart brimming with berries. It also looks stunning sprinkled with a handful of blackberries and sprigs of black or red currants. The pastry, custard and fruit can be prepared in advance, but the tart should be assembled not more than 2 hours before serving, or the pastry will become soggy.**

Preheat the oven to 200°C.

To make the pastry, stir the rice flour, cornflour, ground almonds and salt together in a medium bowl.

Rub the fat into the dry ingredients with your fingertips (or pulse in a processor) until the mixture resembles breadcrumbs. Stir in the sugar. Pour in the beaten egg and bring the pastry together, first with a table knife and then by lightly kneading the dough to a smooth pastry with your hands. Chill the pastry in the fridge for 10–15 minutes.

Roll out and use to line a 24-cm wide tart tin. Blind-bake the tart shell, following the instructions on page 123.

Cool the pastry shell in the tin on a wire rack, then remove the tin and place the pastry shell on a serving dish.

To make the vanilla custard, place the cornflour and sugar in a pan, and mix together with a wooden spoon. Stirring continuously, slowly add the milk to the flour and sugar, to form a smooth, lump-free liquid.

Add the split vanilla pod to the pan and gently heat the custard, stirring continuously, until the custard starts to boil and thicken. The custard may become lumpy, but continue to simmer for a further minute, beating vigorously with a wooden spoon until it becomes smooth and shiny. Remove from the heat and leave to cool. The custard will set as it does so.

When the custard is cool, beat in the cream until the custard is smooth and shiny again. Spread the custard over the base of the pastry shell.

To decorate the tart, first cover the custard with strawberries, hulled end down. Arrange closely together, starting at the edge of the tart and spiralling towards the centre. Scatter over the raspberries, followed by the blueberries. The fruit should completely hide the custard. Just before serving, lightly dust with the icing sugar.

To serve, cut the tart into generous slices with a sharp knife, and lift on to plates with a cake slice.

# PEAR & ALMOND FRANGIPANE TART

**This impressive-looking tart can be made in advance and glazed a few hours before serving.**

Preheat the oven to 180°C.

To make the pastry, stir the rice flour, polenta and salt together in a medium bowl. Rub the fat into the dry ingredients with your fingertips (or pulse in a processor) until the mixture resembles breadcrumbs. Pour in the beaten egg and bring the pastry together, first with a table knife and then by lightly kneading the dough to a smooth pastry with your hands.

Roll out and use to line a 24-cm wide tart tin. Blind-bake the tart shell, following the instructions on page 123.

To make the almond frangipane, place the butter, sugar, eggs, ground almonds and lemon zest in a medium bowl, and whisk together until light and fluffy. Spoon into the pastry shell and even out with a knife. At this stage, the tart can be frozen until required or chilled in the fridge for up to 24 hours before baking. If freezing, completely defrost the tart before topping with fruit.

Peel, halve and core the pears. Arrange the them on top of the filling, with rounded side uppermost and the narrower tip of the pears pointing into the centre. Gently press into the almond mixture to a depth of 1 cm.

Bake the tart in the middle of the oven for 30 minutes, or until the almond frangipane has puffed up around the fruit and is golden brown and springy in the centre. Remove from the oven and leave to cool to room temperature.

Meanwhile, to make the apricot glaze, bring the apricot jam and lemon juice to simmering point in a small pan, stirring until the jam is fully dissolved. Pass through a sieve into a bowl, to remove any pieces of fruit. Leave to cool.

Up to 2 hours before serving, glaze the tart. Check the cooled apricot glaze smoothly coats the back of a spoon. If the glaze is a little thick, thin with 1–2 teaspoons of water or lemon juice. With a pastry brush, generously brush the glaze over the cooked pears and almond filling to give the tart colour and shine.

Cut into generous slices and serve with double cream or ice cream.

- SERVES 6

- FOR THE RICE AND POLENTA PASTRY

110 g rice flour
110 g fine polenta
pinch of salt
110 g cold butter or dairy-free hard baking margarine
1 egg, beaten

- FOR THE FILLING

80 g softened butter
80 g caster sugar
2 eggs
80 g ground almonds
zest of 1 lemon
3 ripe but firm pears

- FOR THE GLAZE

3 tbsp apricot jam
1 tbsp lemon juice

*Tip*

**Try swapping the pears with Granny Smith apples, plums, apricots or rhubarb.**

# FREE-FORM HAZELNUT, PLUM & CINNAMON TART

- SERVES 6–8

- FOR THE HAZELNUT PASTRY

110 g rice flour
55 g cornflour
55 g ground hazelnuts
1 tsp ground cinnamon
pinch of salt
110 g cold butter or dairy-free hard margarine, cut into small pieces
70 g caster sugar
1 egg, beaten

- FOR THE PLUM AND CINNAMON FILLING

500 g plums, stoned and quartered
2 tbsp soft light brown sugar
1 tsp ground cinnamon
zest of 1 orange
1 tbsp ground hazelnuts
1 egg, beaten
large pinch of demerera sugar

**This tart looks charmingly rustic and is robustly flavoured. A really good one for informal meals and fun to make with the children. Try replacing halved plums with sliced nectarines, apricots or apples. For a variation that is quick to make, use a 400 g pack of gluten-free ready-to-roll shortcrust or puff pastry in place of homemade hazelnut pastry.**

Preheat the oven to 190°C.

To make the pastry, stir the rice flour, cornflour, ground hazelnuts, cinnamon and salt together in a medium mixing bowl.

Rub the butter into the dry ingredients with your fingertips (or pulse in a processor) until the mixture resembles breadcrumbs. Stir in the sugar. Pour in the beaten egg and bring the pastry together, first with a table knife and then by lightly kneading the dough to a smooth pastry with your hands.

Between sheets of cling film, roll out the pastry into a circle approximately 25 cm wide and 3 mm thick, and transfer to a large shallow roasting tin.

Mix the plums, sugar, cinnamon, orange zest and ground hazelnuts together. Heap into the centre of the pastry, leaving a 5-cm border around the edge.

Draw the edge of the pastry circle up over the fruit, pleating and pinching the pastry to form a leak proof 'bowl' to hold the cooked plum juice.

Brush the pastry with beaten egg and sprinkle with the demerara sugar.

Bake the tart in the oven for 40 minutes, or until the tart is golden and crisp and the centre of the pastry base is cooked.

Using 2 fish slices, transfer the tart to a serving dish. To serve, slice into generous wedges and serve with vanilla ice cream.

# TARTE TATIN

- SERVES 4

1 x 400-g pack gluten-free puff pastry, defrosted

- FOR THE CARAMEL

80 g caster sugar
30 g unsalted butter, diced

- FOR THE FILLING

8 Granny Smith apples
30 g unsalted butter, diced
1 tsp ground cinnamon
60 g caster sugar

**One of the most delicious puddings in existence. You will need a 20 cm frying pan with an ovenproof handle because the tart is transferred from the hob to the oven for baking.**

Preheat the oven to 200°C.

To make the filling, first make the caramel. Put the sugar in a medium frying pan, and place over a medium heat. When the sugar has dissolved and browned to a rich caramel colour, turn off the heat and carefully swirl in the diced butter.

Meanwhile, peel and core the apples. Cut 4 of the apples into halves and the remaining 4 apples into quarters. You will end up with 8 halves and 16 quarters.

Cover the caramel in the pan with the apples by leaning the rounded sides of the apple halves against the curved sides of the frying pan, then arrange the quartered apples in the centre, curved side down. Pack them in tightly, making sure that there are no gaps between the apples.

Dot the apples with the diced butter, then mix the cinnamon and sugar together and sprinkle over the apples. Bake in the oven for 20 minutes, or until the apples are tender.

Roll out the pastry into a square 3 mm thick and cut into a circle at least 4 cm wider than the rim of the frying pan. Cover the sugared apples with the circle of pastry, tucking the edges down between the apples and the sides of the pan, being careful not to burn yourself. Return to the oven for a further 30 minutes, or until the puff pastry is crisp and golden.

Remove the tart from the oven and leave to cool for 30 minutes.

Place a large serving dish with a rim over the frying pan. Holding the plate and pan firmly together, quickly flip the pan over to turn out the tart onto the plate with the apples uppermost, being careful not to lose any of the precious apple caramel. Before lifting the frying pan off the serving plate, sharply tap the frying pan on the base and around the sides to loosen any apple sticking to it. The apples should be a dark caramel colour, smooth and shiny.

Serve with double cream or vanilla ice cream.

# LEMON MERINGUE PIE

**A traditional and spectacular favourite for a special occasion. The pie shell is generously filled with sharp lemon custard to complement the mallowy meringue piled high on top.**

- SERVES 4–6

- FOR THE RICE AND ALMOND PASTRY

110 g rice flour
55 g cornflour
55 g ground almonds
pinch of salt
110 g cold butter or dairy-free hard baking margarine, cut into small pieces
70 g caster sugar
1 egg, beaten

- FOR THE LEMON FILLING

2 level tbsp cornflour
55 g caster sugar
290 ml milk or dairy-free milk
zest and juice of 2 lemons
2 egg yolks

- FOR THE MERINGUE TOPPING

3 medium eggs, separated and brought to room temperature
½ tsp cream of tartar
pinch of fine salt
175 g caster sugar
1 tsp cornflour

To make the pastry, rub the fat into the dry ingredients with your fingertips (or pulse in a food processor) until the mixture resembles breadcrumbs. Stir in the sugar. Pour in the beaten egg and bring the pastry together into a smooth ball with your hands.

Roll out and use to line a 24-cm wide tart tin. Blind-bake the tart shell, following the instructions on page 123. Cool the pastry case in the tin on a wire rack and reduce the oven temperature to 150°C.

To make the lemon filling, mix the cornflour and sugar with 3 tablespoons of the milk until smooth. Bring the remaining milk to a simmer in the pan then stir into the cornflour mixture. Pour back into the pan and bring slowly to the boil, stirring continuously. The mixture will suddenly thicken and become lumpy. Continue to boil for 1 minute, beating with a wooden spoon until smooth.

Stir the lemon zest and lemon juice into the thickened milk mixture to cool, then beat in the egg yolks. Pour the lemon filling into the blind-baked pastry base.

To make the meringue, place the egg whites in a large bowl and whisk on low speed for 30 seconds to create a loose froth. Add the cream of tartar and salt, and continue to whisk on a high speed until the meringue thickens and forms soft peaks. Whisk in half of the caster sugar at high speed, adding a tablespoon at a time, until the meringue is stiff and glossy. Mix the remaining sugar with the cornflour, sprinkle over the meringue and fold in with a large metal spoon.

Pile the meringue on top of the lemon filling right to the edges, to seal the tart. Tease the meringue into peaks with the back of a fork.

Bake the pie in the oven for 35 minutes, or until the meringue has lightly browned but is still mallowy and soft inside.

Gently remove the sides of the tart tin and cool on a wire rack. Slide the pie onto a serving plate and serve in generous slices with double cream.

# CLASSIC APPLE PIE

- SERVES 4–6

- FOR THE BUCKWHEAT AND ALMOND PASTRY

110 g buckwheat flour
110 g rice flour
110 g cornflour
110 g ground almonds
pinch of salt
220 g cold butter
70 g caster sugar
1 egg, beaten

- FOR THE FILLING

1 kg Bramley or Granny Smith apples, peeled, cored and cut into bite-sizes chunks
4 tbsp caster sugar
1 tbsp cinnamon (optional)
1 egg, beaten, for glazing
caster sugar, for sprinkling

**Use firm, tart apples such as Bramley, Cox's or Granny Smith for apple pie. To make apple and blackberry pie, replace 200 g of the apple with blackberries. Alternatively, replace the apples entirely with an equal quantity of other robustly flavoured fruits such as cherries, plums and gooseberries.**

Preheat the oven to 180°C.

To make the pastry, sift the flours, ground almonds and salt into a bowl. Rub the butter into the flour with your fingertips (or pulse in a processor) until the mixture resembles breadcrumbs. Stir (or pulse) in the sugar, followed by the beaten egg, until the pastry comes together in a ball. Gently knead the pastry until it forms a smooth ball and divide in two.

Place one half of the pastry between 2 sheets of cling film, and roll out to 3 mm thick. Peel away the top sheets of cling film, then turn the pastry over and ease the pastry into a 1-litre pie dish to line it. Gently push the pastry against the sides, corner and bottom, leaving the pastry hanging over the pie dish rim. Remove the second sheet of cling film.

To make the filling, mix the apple with the sugar and tip into the pastry-lined pie dish. Spread out the apples keeping some height in the centre.

Roll out the remaining pastry to the same thickness as the first half. Remove the first sheet of cling film and cover the apples, with the edges hanging over the edge of the pie dish. With a sharp knife or pair of scissors, trim the overhanging edges to 2 cm, then pinch the overhanging pastry from the base and lid together with your thumb and forefingers, to form a scalloped edge around the pie. With a sharp knife, make a small hole in the centre to allow steam to escape.

Brush the top of the pie with beaten egg, decorate with shapes made from the pastry trimmings and sprinkle with caster sugar. Bake in the oven for 45–60 minutes until the pastry is golden and crisp, and the apples are tender when tested with a skewer.

Remove from the oven and leave to cool for 5 minutes. Serve generous slices with vanilla ice cream, double cream or custard.

*Tip*

**To make in advance, assemble the pie, cover with cling film and chill in the fridge for up to 24 hours before baking. To save time, use 2 x 400g blocks of defrosted ready-to-roll gluten-free shortcrust pastry in place of the buckwheat and almond pastry above.**

## INDIVIDUAL CHRISTMAS MINCE PIES

**A must for Christmas. Serve warm with a cup of tea or coffee, or for dessert with vanilla ice cream or brandy butter. Make with the buckwheat and almond pastry recipe opposite or with gluten-free ready-to-roll defrosted sweet or savoury shortcrust pastry. For flaky mince pies, use puff pastry for the pie lids.**

Preheat the oven to 200°C.

Roll out half the pastry, between 2 sheets of cling film. to 2 mm thick. Peel off 1 sheet and turn the pastry down on a work surface lightly floured with rice flour.

Using a pastry cutter 8 cm across, cut out 18 circles of pastry and gently press into 18 holes of two 12-hole cupcake tins. You may have to bring the pastry together and roll again to obtain 18 circles.

Spoon 2 teaspoons of mincemeat into each pie base.

Roll out the second pastry dough into a circle 2 mm thick. Using a second pastry cutter, 6 cm across, cut out another 18 circles and centre them on top of the mincemeat, pressing the edges of the pastry base and lid together. With a sharp knife, make a small slit in the centre of each lid, to allow steam to escape during baking.

Brush the pies with beaten egg, and bake in the oven for 20 minutes, or until the pies are crisp and golden brown.

Loosen the edge of the pies from the tin with a table knife, and transfer to a wire rack to cool for 10 minutes. Serve lightly dusted with icing sugar.

## INDIVIDUAL APPLE PIES

To make 18 individual apple pies, make the pastry as described opposite. Roll out to 2–3 mm thick and cut into rounds with a large 8-cm pastry cutter. Preheat the oven to 200°C. Line 18 holes of two 12-hole muffin trays.

Peel and core 4 Granny Smith apples, and cut into 1-cm dice. Mix the diced apple with 2 tablespoons of caster sugar and fill each pie base.

Roll out the pastry again, and cut out 18 more 8-cm rounds. Use to cover the apple, sealing the pastry around the edges.

Brush each apple pie with beaten egg, then sprinkle with demerara sugar. Bake in the oven for 20–30 minutes. Leave to cool in the tins for 5 minutes, then transfer to a wire rack to cool.

# GATEAU PITHIVIER WITH ORANGE & DARK CHOCOLATE

**This traditional French puff pastry and almond frangipane pie, originating from the town of Pithivier in Northern France, was introduced to me when I trained at Leiths School of Food and Wine in London. It is a rich and luscious dessert to serve for a special occasion. It is best served warm with crème fraîche, vanilla ice cream or simply with double cream.**

- SERVES 6–8

2 x 400-g packs gluten-free puff pastry, defrosted to room temperature

- FOR THE FRANGIPANE FILLING

100 g unsalted butter, softened
100 g caster sugar
1 egg
100 g almonds, ground
1 tbsp cornflour
zest of 1 orange
1 tbsp Cointreau
30 g dark chocolate chips

1 egg, beaten, to glaze

Preheat the oven to 220°C.

To make the frangipane filling, place the butter, sugar, eggs, ground almonds, cornflour, orange zest and Cointreau in a bowl. Whisk them together until light and creamy, then fold in the chocolate chips.

Roll out the first block of puff pastry into a large rectangle 2 mm thick. Using a pan lid or plate, cut out a circle 20 cm across with a sharp knife. Place the circle in a large shallow roasting tin.

Spoon the frangipane filling into the centre of the pastry circle. Flatten out, leaving a 3-cm border around the edge. Brush the border with a little beaten egg.

Roll out the second block of pastry into a rectangle 3 mm thick, and this time cut out a circle 25 cm across. Use this to cover the almond filling, then gently press the pastry edges together. Brush the pie lid with more of the beaten egg and gently score a spiral pattern on the lid with the back of a small sharp knife, being careful not to puncture the pastry.

Bake the pie in the middle of the oven for 30–40 minutes until risen, crisp and golden brown. Check to see that the centre of the pastry base is golden and crisp, too, before removing from the oven.

Transfer the pie to a serving dish, and keep warm until you are ready to serve.

With a sharp knife, slice the Pithivier and serve with double cream or vanilla ice cream.

*Tip*

**The uncooked pie can be made and stored in the fridge 24 hours in advance, then baked an hour or so before eating.**

# CHERRY LATTICE PIE

- SERVES 6–8

- FOR THE BUCKWHEAT AND ALMOND PASTRY

110 g buckwheat flour
55 g cornflour
55 g ground almonds
pinch of salt
110 g cold butter, diced
70 g caster sugar
½–1 egg, beaten

- FOR THE CHERRY FILLING

450 g frozen dark sweet cherries
60 g ground almonds
3 tbsp caster sugar
1 tsp ground cinnamon
finely grated zest of 1 lemon
1 tbsp cornflour
1 medium egg, beaten, to glaze
1 tbsp demerara sugar, to decorate

Tip

**Replacing the lattice pastry with a crumble topping (page 152) makes a great variation on a theme.**

**An attractive traditional pie perfect for eating warm on a winter's day or cold on a picnic. The buckwheat and almond pastry is rich and biscuity, contrasting perfectly with filling. Serve with custard, double cream or vanilla ice cream.**

Preheat the oven to 200°C. Put a baking sheet in the oven to heat.

To make the pastry, sift the flour, ground almonds and salt into a bowl. Rub the butter into the flour with your fingertips (or pulse in a processor) until the mixture resembles breadcrumbs. Stir (or pulse) in the sugar, followed by half of the egg, then a little more at a time, until the pastry comes together in a ball. Gently knead the pastry until it forms a smooth ball.

Place between 2 sheets of cling film and roll out the pastry to 3 mm thick. Remove the top sheet of cling film, and use the pastry to line a 1-litre pie dish or 23-cm loose-bottomed tart tin. Pass the rolling pin over the dish or tart tin to neaten the edges, then peel away the second sheet of cling film.

Blind-bake in the oven for 20 minutes, following the instructions on page 123. Remove the greaseproof paper and return the pastry to the oven for a further 10 minutes, or until the pastry is crisp and light golden.

Reduce the oven temperature to 180°C.

Meanwhile, to make the filling mix together the cherries, ground almonds, sugar, cinnamon, lemon zest and cornflour. Tip into the blind-baked pastry shell and spread out evenly.

Using cornflour for dusting, roll out the remaining pastry and cut into long strips, about 5 mm wide. Weave the strips together over the pie filling to form a lattice pattern. Brush the ends of the lattice strips with water, and gently press into place on the pie base. Brush the lattice with the beaten egg glaze, and sprinkle with the demerara sugar.

Transfer the pie to the hot baking sheet, and bake for 50–60 minutes until the pastry lattice is golden and the cherry filling is gently bubbling.

# HAZELNUT MERINGUE PEACH MELBA CAKE WITH RASPBERRY SAUCE

**The gentle nuttiness of hazelnuts and the retro pairing of peaches and raspberries complement the meringue perfectly. A colourful and impressive dessert for special occasions.**

- SERVES 6

- FOR THE HAZELNUT MERINGUE

100 g blanched hazelnuts
3 medium eggs, separated and brought to room temperature
½ tsp cream of tartar
pinch of fine salt
175 g caster sugar
1 tsp cornflour

- FOR THE PEACH MELBA FILLING

1 heaped tbsp icing sugar
300 ml double cream
2 or 3 ripe yellow peaches, peeled, stoned, quartered and thinly sliced lengthways
100 g raspberries

- FOR THE RASPBERRY SAUCE

250 g ripe raspberries
2 tbsp caster sugar

Preheat the oven to 180°C.

Place the hazelnuts on a baking tray and roast in the oven for 5 minutes, or until golden brown. Tip the nuts into a dish and leave to cool completely before grinding to breadcrumb consistency.

Next, line a large baking sheet with greaseproof paper. Using a pan lid or plate about 20 cm across, draw 2 circles on a piece of greaseproof paper, then turn the paper over and place on the baking tray.

To make the meringue, put the egg whites in a large bowl and whisk on low speed for 30 seconds to create a loose froth. Add the cream of tartar and salt, and whisk on high speed until the meringue thickens and forms soft peaks that wobble when shaken. Whisk in half of the caster sugar at high speed, adding a tablespoon at a time, until the meringue is stiff and glossy. Mix the remaining sugar with the cornflour and cooled hazelnuts, then sprinkle over the meringue. Fold in with a large metal spoon until just blended. Be careful not to over mix, or the meringue will collapse.

Divide the meringue evenly between the 2 circles drawn on the greaseproof paper, and spread out to just inside the perimeter. Bake the meringue for 40 minutes, or until it is firm, golden brown and easily peels away from the greaseproof paper. Cool on a wire rack.

To make the raspberry sauce, blend the raspberries and sugar until smooth then pass through a fine sieve into a bowl. Pour into a serving jug, cover and chill, until required.

In a separate bowl, sift the icing sugar into the double cream. Whisk on medium speed until the cream just holds its shape.

To assemble the meringue cake, place a meringue disc, flat side down on a serving plate. Spread on half the cream with a palette knife, and scatter over two-thirds of the peaches and raspberries. Cover with the second disc, flat side down. Spread with the other half of the cream, and scatter over the remaining peach slices and raspberries.

Serve in generous slices with raspberry sauce.

# MERINGUE KISSES WITH PASSION FRUIT CREAM & MANGO

- SERVES 4

- FOR THE MERINGUE KISSES

2 egg whites
pinch of salt
110 g caster sugar

- FOR THE PASSION FRUIT CREAM

200 ml double cream
1½ tbsp icing sugar
5 passion fruits
1 large ripe mango, cut into thin slices lengthways

**The delicate flavours of meringue and passion fruit cream complement each other perfectly, and the mango and lime provide a fruity zing. For a variation, make a passion fruit and mango pavlova. Spread the meringue out into a circle 20 cm in diameter and then bake as described for the meringue kisses. Top with passion fruit cream, sliced mango and passion fruit seeds.**

Preheat the oven to 110°C, and line a baking sheet with greaseproof paper.

In a clean, dry bowl, whisk the egg whites with a pinch of salt to straight, stiff peaks that do not wobble when the bowl is shaken from side to side.

Sprinkle half of the sugar over the egg whites, and continue to whisk until the meringue is very stiff and glossy. Fold in the remaining sugar with a large metal spoon.

Drop heaped dessertspoons of meringue onto the greaseproof paper, keeping them at least 3 cm apart to allow for spreading.

Bake in the oven for 1–1½ hours until they peel away easily from the greaseproof paper. Transfer to a wire rack to cool.

To make the passion fruit cream, whip the cream and icing sugar until it just holds its shape. Halve 3 of the passion fruits, and scoop the pulp into a small bowl. Fold into the the cream, which will thicken as the fruit is stirred through it.

To serve, sandwich 4 heaped dessertspoons of passion fruit cream between 2 meringue kisses, and arrange on 4 plates with the mango slices. Top with the pulp scooped out of the remaining passion fruit.

# APRICOT & ORANGE BREAD & BUTTER PUDDING

- SERVES 6

1 tbsp raisins
1 tbsp dried apricots, thinly sliced
1 tbsp mixed peel
125 ml Cointreau or freshly squeezed orange juice
55 g butter or dairy-free margarine, softened
400 g gluten-free sliced white bread, crusts removed
300 ml whole milk or dairy-free milk
300 ml double cream or soya cream
1 vanilla pod, split lengthways
finely grated of 1 orange
3 large eggs
110 g caster sugar
2–3 tbsp apricot jam
icing sugar for dusting

**Bread and butter pudding made with gluten-free bread is delicate and light, and you and your family will want to make this recipe over and over again.**

Soak the raisins, apricots and mixed peel in the Cointreau.

Preheat the oven to 170°C.

Butter the bread and cut each slice in half on the diagonal. Arrange in a 1-litre ovenproof dish, greased with butter or dairy-free margarine.

Pour the milk and cream into a pan, and bring to a simmer with the vanilla pod and orange zest. Whisk the eggs and sugar together, then stir in the hot milk mixture. Scrape the vanilla seeds into this custard and discard the pod.

Sprinkle the soaked raisins, mixed peel and any remaining Cointreau over the bread, then pour over the custard.

Place the dish in a roasting tray on the middle shelf of the oven. Being careful not to splash the pudding, pour water into the roasting tray to halfway up the ovenproof dish. Gently push the roasting tray into the middle of the shelf and bake the pudding for 35 minutes, or until lightly set and golden brown.

To finish, gently heat the apricot jam over a low heat and brush over the baked pudding. Dust with icing sugar before serving.

*Tip*

**For a slightly richer version, replace the gluten-free bread with thinly sliced gluten-free brioche. Alternatively, for some spice, use spiced fruit loaf.**

# SUMMER PUDDING

**The archetypal English dessert, brimming with soft fruits and colour. This dessert looks harder to make than it really is. Go on, have a go. The effort is worth it.**

- SERVES 6

1 kg mixed strawberries, raspberries, redcurrants, blackcurrants, blackberries and black cherries
3 tbsp water
170 g caster sugar
2 strips of orange zest
2 strips of lemon zest
8–10 slices of gluten-free white bread, crusts removed

Place the fruit, water, sugar, orange and lemon zest in a pan. Mix well and bring to the boil. Simmer for 1 minute and leave to cool.

Cut a circle from 1 slice of bread, to fit the base of a 1-litre pudding bowl. Cut the remaining slices in half, on the diagonal.

When the fruit is nearly cold, tip into a sieve, placed over a bowl to collect the juice.

Dip the prepared bread circle and triangles into the juice, then use to line the bottom and sides of the bowl, leaving no gaps.

Spoon in the fruit, and cover the top with the remaining triangles of bread, first dipped in juice. Trim any bread hanging over the rim of the bowl with a knife.

Stand the pudding basin in a dish, place a small plate on top of the pudding and weigh down with a 400-g tin. Chill in the fridge overnight to set.

Meanwhile, return the remaining juice to the pan and boil until glossy and syrupy. Leave to cool, cover and chill until needed.

To serve the pudding, remove the plate and weight. Place a serving plate over the rim of the pudding basin and quickly turn them over. Holding firmly onto the plate and basin, give them a sharp shake and repeat until you feel the pudding loosen inside the bowl. Lift the inverted bowl off the pudding. Pour over the reserved fruit syrup, and serve with a jug of thick pouring cream.

*Tip*

**For a richer version, replace the bread with thinly silced gluten-free brioche or Madeira cake.**

# STICKY DATE & TOFFEE PUDDING

- SERVES 4–6

- FOR THE STICKY DATE SPONGE

250 g chopped dates
300 ml hot black tea, traditional or Earl Grey
100 g butter or dairy-free baking margarine, softened
170 g muscovado sugar
4 eggs
110 g rice flour
55 g ground almonds
55 g cornflour
1 tsp baking powder
1 tsp mixed spice
½ tsp instant coffee powder

- FOR THE TOFFEE SAUCE

90 g unsalted butter or dairy-free margarine
110 g muscovado sugar
140 g double cream or dairy-free soya cream
pinch of salt
1 tbsp dark rum (optional)

**Since we've been living in Scotland, this very rich and comforting dessert has become a family favourite pudding after the Sunday roast on cold winter days, particularly when there is little to do afterwards. Delicious served with a scoop of vanilla ice cream.**

Preheat the oven to 180°C. Grease a 2-lb loaf tin or a 1-litre ovenproof dish well with butter or diary-free baking margarine.

Place the dates in a bowl and cover with hot tea. Leave to soak for 15–30 minutes.

To make the sponge, whisk the butter, muscovado sugar, eggs, rice flour, almonds, cornflour, baking powder, mixed spice and instant coffee powder together in a medium bowl.

Drain the tea-soaked dates, and whiz to a purée in a food processor, then fold into the sponge mixture. Spoon the sponge mixture into the prepared baking dish, and bake in the middle of the oven for 30–40 minutes. Remove from the oven when the sponge has risen and feels firm and springy in the centre when gently pressed.

Meanwhile, make the toffee sauce by placing the butter, sugar and cream in a pan. Stirring continuously over a low heat, bring the ingredients to a simmer. Continue to stir until the sugar has dissolved and the sauce has thickened to coating consistency. Stir in the rum, if using.

Spoon the sponge pudding into warm bowls, and serve with the toffee sauce.

# SELF-SAUCING RICH CHOCOLATE MOCHA PUDDING

**This is the epitome of a weekend pudding to enjoy with friends and family. You may have to make two, as people are bound to come back for seconds.**

- SERVES 6

- FOR THE CHOCOLATE SPONGE

60 g butter or dairy-free margarine softened
170 g muscovado sugar
5 medium eggs
70 g rice flour
70 g ground almonds
30 g cocoa powder
2 tsp baking powder
pinch of salt

- FOR THE CHOCOLATE MOCHA SAUCE

100 g soft light brown sugar
100 g muscovado sugar
1 tbsp cocoa powder
250 ml fresh strong black coffee

Preheat the oven to 180°C. Grease a deep 1-litre ovenproof dish with butter or dairy-free baking margarine. A soufflé dish works very well.

To make the chocolate sponge, in a medium bowl, whisk all the sponge ingredients together until smooth. Pour the mixture into the greased ovenproof dish.

To make the sauce, mix the light and dark brown sugars and cocoa powder together in the bottom of a small pan. Stir in the hot black coffee. Bring the coffee mixture to a simmer, and stir until the sugar has fully dissolved.

Pour the chocolate mocha sauce over the chocolate sponge mixture, and immediately place the pudding on the centre shelf of the oven. Bake for 30 minutes, or until the sponge has risen and is firm in the centre and the sauce is bubbling around the sides.

Spoon into warm bowls, and serve with cream or vanilla ice cream.

# RHUBARB, ORANGE & GINGER CRUMBLE WITH HOMEMADE VANILLA CUSTARD

- SERVES 4

800 g rhubarb stems, sliced across into 5-cm lengths
4 tbsp light brown sugar
1 tsp ground ginger
zest and juice of 1 orange

- FOR THE CRUMBLE TOPPING

110 g rice flour or ground almonds
100 g gluten-free rolled oats
pinch of salt
100 g demerara sugar
110 g butter or dairy-free baking margarine, softened

- FOR THE CUSTARD

500 ml whole milk or dairy-free milk
1 tbsp caster sugar
1 vanilla pod, split lengthways
2 tsp cornflour
3 egg yolks

- VARIATION: PLUM, ORANGE AND CINNAMON CRUMBLE

Replace the rhubarb with 900 g plums, halved and stoned, and the ginger with 1tsp ground cinnamon if you prefer. Serve with vanilla ice cream or homemade vanilla custard, see recipe above.

**Rhubarb and custard – a classic British combination – is enhanced with a hint of orange and ginger. Serve the custard recipe below with Classic Apple Pie (page 140). This crumble is also delicious with plums or apples in place of the rhubarb.**

Preheat the oven to 200°C.

Mix the rhubarb with the orange zest, light brown sugar and ground ginger. Tip the rhubarb mixture into a 1-litre ovenproof serving dish at least 5 cm deep. Pour over the orange juice.

To make the crumble, first mix the rice flour, oats, salt and demerara sugar together in a large bowl. Rub the butter into the dry ingredients with the tips of your fingers (or pulse in a food processor) until the mixture looks like coarse breadcrumbs. Sprinkle the crumble over the rhubarb and bake in the oven for 30–40 minutes until the crumble topping is crisp and golden brown, and the rhubarb is soft and gently bubbling around the edge of the dish.

Meanwhile, make the custard. Place the milk, sugar and vanilla pod in a medium pan, slowly bring to a simmer. Remove from the heat and set aside for 30 minutes to allow the vanilla flavour to infuse the milk. Scrape the seeds from the vanilla pod into the milk, and discard the pod.

Mix the cornflour with 2 tablespoons of the vanilla-infused milk until fully dispersed then stir into the pan of vanilla-infused milk. Return the milk to a simmer, stirring continuously, over a gentle heat. Simmer for 3 minutes to slightly thicken the milk. Remove from the heat.

Beat the egg yolks in a mixing bowl, and stir the hot, thickened milk into the beaten yolks in a thin, steady stream. The sauce should thicken to coat the back of a spoon. If still a little thin, pour the custard back into the pan and gently simmer over a low heat, stirring continuously, until the sauce reaches the required consistency. Remove from the heat.

Once the crumble is baked, remove from the oven and allow to cool for 10 minutes, then spoon into warm bowls and serve with the warm custard.

# APRICOT CLAFOUTIS

- SERVES 4–6

200 ml whole milk or dairy-free milk
200 ml whipping cream or soya cream
1 vanilla pod, split lengthways
3 medium eggs
100 g caster sugar, plus 1 tbsp extra
1 heaped tbsp cornflour
30 g unsalted butter or dairy-free margarine
500 g ripe apricots, halved and stoned
1 tbsp demerara sugar for sprinkling

**This family-friendly batter pudding is a traditional dessert from the French region of Limousin. Clafoutis is usually made with ripe black cherries, but is just as delicious made with rhubarb, plums, apricots, berries and apples, so have fun experimenting with different fruit.**

Preheat the oven to 180°C.

Place the milk, cream and vanilla pod in a small pan, and slowly bring to a simmer over a low heat. Remove from the heat.

In a medium bowl, beat the eggs, the 100 g caster sugar and cornflour together with a wooden spoon, then gradually stir in the hot milk mixture to form a smooth batter. Discard the vanilla pod.

Place the butter in a 1-litre ovenproof dish, and heat in the oven for 5 minutes. Mix the apricots with the extra sugar. Remove the buttered ovenproof dish from the oven, scatter the apricots over the bottom and toss in the butter. Turn the apricots cut side up, return to the oven and bake for 5 minutes. Open the oven door, pull the dish towards you and carefully pour the batter around the apricots.

Bake the clafoutis in the oven for 30 minutes until the batter is just set in the middle. Sprinkle with the demerara sugar, and serve hot with double cream.

# NEW YORK VANILLA BAKED CHEESECAKE

**This cheesecake recipe is perfect eaten as it is or paired with summer berries and runny honey or Spiced Blueberry Compote (page 25).**

• SERVES 6–8

80 g gluten-free sweet plain biscuits such as oat biscuits, rich tea or digestives
50 g butter
450 g full-fat soft cream cheese
1 heaped tbsp cornflour
finely grated zest of 1 lemon
1 tsp vanilla essence
100 g caster sugar
2 medium eggs, separated
100 ml crème fraîche

Preheat the oven to 180°C. Lightly grease a 20-cm springform cake tin with vegetable oil, and line the bottom with disc of greaseproof paper, lightly brushed with a little more oil.

Crush the biscuits in a plastic bag, with a rolling pin, to the consistency of fine breadcrumbs.

Melt the butter and stir in the crushed biscuits. Spread over the bottom of the cake tin, and press into an even layer with your fingers or the back of a spoon.

Bake in the oven for 10 minutes, or until golden brown and crisp, then leave to cool. Reduce the oven temperature to 150°C.

In a large bowl, beat together the cream cheese, cornflour, lemon zest, vanilla essence, sugar, egg yolks and crème fraîche until smooth.

Whisk the egg whites in a separate bowl until they make soft peaks that slightly wobble when the bowl is shaken. Stir 1 heaped tablespoon of egg white into the cream cheese mixture to loosen it. Gently fold in the remaining egg white to form a foamy mixture.

Pour the cream cheese mixture over the biscuit base, and bake in the oven for 45–60 minutes, or until the cheesecake is just set in the centre and turning slightly golden.

Transfer to a wire rack and leave to cool in the tin. Once cold, store in the fridge, covered with cling film, for 24 hours. Before removing the cheesecake from the tin, carefully run a sharp knife around the edge.

Transfer to a serving plate and serve in generous slices with summer berries and drizzled with honey or with Spiced Blueberry Compote.

# Home Baking

Fill your home with the smell of baking by trying one of my muffin, scone, cake or biscuit recipes. Sample something a little unusual such as my Chocolate, Beetroot & Raspberry Cupcakes, or my Savoury Cheese Sablés – perfect with drinks – or produce a showstopper such as my Whisked Sponge Filled with Cream and Strawberries.

# MUFFINS

**As you'll see from the ingredients below, you can make savoury or sweet muffins with a range of different flours. Glazed Orange and Poppy Seed Muffins are a firm favourite with my sons, and the savoury muffins are delicious served warm with soups and salads.**

## ROAST BUTTERNUT SQUASH, RED PEPPER, GOAT'S CHEESE, PINE NUT & THYME MUFFINS

**These savoury muffins, full of colour, flavour and texture, are delicious served warm.**

MAKES 12 LARGE MUFFINS

- 1 tbsp olive oil
- 125 g butternut squash, peeled, seeded and cut into 1-cm dice
- 125 g red pepper, deseeded and cut into 1-cm dice
- 80 g fine polenta
- 100 g cornflour
- 100 g rice flour
- 4 tsp gluten-free baking powder
- 1 tbsp thyme leaves
- 6 large eggs, at room temperature
- 150 g butter, melted
- 150 g goat's cheese, cut into 1-cm dice
- 40 g pine nuts
- salt and freshly ground black pepper

Preheat the oven to 180°C. Place 12 large muffin cases in a 12-hole muffin tin.

Drizzle the olive oil over the butternut squash and red pepper, then season with a pinch of salt and pepper and roast for 20 minutes. Leave to cool.

In a large bowl, mix together the polenta, cornflour, rice flour, baking powder, a large pinch of salt, 4 grinds of black pepper and the thyme leaves.

In a separate bowl, beat the eggs and melted butter together, and beat into the dry ingredients to form a smooth batter.

Stir the cooled roasted butternut squash and peppers, goat's cheese and pine nuts into the batter, then spoon the batter into the paper cases until three-quarters full. Bake in the middle of the oven for 40 minutes, or until the centre of the muffins spring back when gently pressed and are golden on top.

Leave to cool in the tray for 5 minutes and serve warm, or turn out onto a wired rack to cool completely.

These muffins will keep for 3 days stored in an airtight container in the fridge. To serve, warm through for 10 minutes in an oven preheated to 160°C.

## GLAZED ORANGE & POPPY SEED MUFFINS

**These fruity muffins are delicious for breakfast. Try swapping the orange with lemon, or add a large handful of berries in place of the poppy seeds for variety.**

MAKES 12 LARGE MUFFINS

- 150 g rice flour
- 150 g cornflour
- 75 g ground almonds
- 160 g golden caster sugar
- 1 heaped tbsp poppy seeds
- 3 tsp gluten-free baking powder
- pinch of salt
- 125 g unsalted butter or dairy-free baking margarine
- 6 medium eggs, lightly whisked
- grated zest of 2 oranges
- 80 ml freshly squeezed orange juice

FOR THE ORANGE GLAZE

- 1 tbsp orange juice
- 3 tbsp icing sugar
- 1 tbsp poppy seeds

Preheat the oven to 190°C, and place 12 large muffin cases in a 12-hole large muffin tray.

Mix the rice flour, cornflour, ground almonds, sugar, poppy seeds, baking powder and salt together in a large bowl.

Melt the butter in a pan and stir into the beaten eggs. Stir in the orange zest and juice.

Beat the egg and orange mixture into the dry ingredients until the batter becomes smooth.

Fill the muffin cases until three-quarters full, and bake in centre of the oven for 20–25 minutes until the muffins are well risen in the centre and a skewer inserted into the muffin centre, comes out clean. Transfer the muffins to a wire rack to cool.

Meanwhile, make the orange glaze by stirring the orange juice into the icing sugar to form a smooth icing. Drizzle over the muffins and sprinkle with the poppy seeds.

These muffins are best eaten really fresh but can be eaten within 2–3 days if they are stored in an airtight container.

## SPICED APPLE, DATE & WALNUT MUFFINS

**These easy-to-make muffins are delicious straight out of the oven.**

MAKES 14–16 LARGE MUFFINS

- 3 Granny Smith apples, peeled, cored, quartered and cut into 1-cm dice
- 150 g chopped dates
- 60 g walnuts, roughly chopped
- 100 g rice flour
- 50 g cornflour
- 50 g ground almonds
- 1 tsp gluten-free baking powder
- 200 g golden caster sugar
- 1 tsp ground cinnamon
- 1 tsp mixed spice
- 125 g butter or dairy-free baking margarine
- 6 medium eggs

Preheat the oven to 180°C, and place 14–16 large muffin cases in two 12-hole muffin trays.

Mix the apples, dates and walnuts together.

In a large bowl, sift in the rice flour, cornflour, ground almonds and baking powder. Stir in the caster sugar, ground cinnamon and mixed spice. Add the diced butter and eggs and beat the ingredients together until smooth. Mix in the apple mixture.

Spoon the mixture into the paper cases until three-quarters full.

Bake the muffins in the oven for 20 minutes, or until set and springy in the centre.

Eat warm, straight out of the oven, or cooled and store in an airtight container for up to 2 days.

# SULTANA & SPICE SCONES

- MAKES 6

110 g potato flour
110 g cornflour
3 tsp gluten-free baking powder
½ tsp salt
1 tbsp golden caster sugar
1 tsp mixed spice
55 g cold butter or dairy-free hard baking margarine, cut into small pieces
2 medium eggs mixed with milk, or dairy-free milk, to make up to 120 ml
60 g sultanas
milk or beaten egg to glaze the scones

**These scones taste at their best served warm, straight from the oven, with unsalted butter or whipped cream and strawberry jam.**

Preheat the oven to 220°C.

Sift the potato flour, cornflour, baking powder, salt, sugar and spice into a large mixing bowl.

With your fingertips, rub the butter into the flour until the mixture looks like coarse breadcrumbs.

Beat the egg and milk mixture together, and stir into the flour mixture with a table knife. Add the sultanas and gently knead the dough on a lightly floured work surface until smooth.

Working quickly, roll out the dough to 2.5 cm. Cut into rounds with a 5-cm plain or fluted round pastry cutter. Bring any spare dough together and roll out once again to cut out more scones.

Place the scones on a floured baking sheet, brush the tops with a little milk and bake in the centre of the oven for 10 minutes, or until risen and golden on the top and bottom.

Serve the scones straight from the oven or cool on a wire rack. Serve within 2–3 hours to enjoy them at their best. Alternatively, freeze when cool. Defrost when needed, just before eating, refresh in a hot oven for 10 minutes.

# CHEESE, BACON & GRAINY MUSTARD SCONES

**These delicious savoury scones make a great accompaniment for soup and salads, or can be served with cheese and cold meats. Use a good-quality wholegrain mustard and mature Cheddar cheese.**

- MAKES 6

4 streaky bacon rashers, sliced across very thinly
½ tbsp olive oil
110 g potato flour
110 g cornflour
2 tsp gluten-free baking powder
pinch of salt
freshly gournd black pepper
50 g cold butter, cut into small pieces
60 g mature Cheddar cheese, coarsely grated
2 medium eggs mixed with milk to make up to 120 ml
2 tsp wholegrain mustard
cornflour
milk, to glaze
1 tbsp grated Cheddar cheese

Preheat the oven to 220°C.

Fry the bacon in the oil until golden brown.

Sift the potato flour, cornflour, baking powder, salt and black pepper into a large bowl.

With your fingertips, rub the butter and cheese into the flour until the mixture looks like coarse breadcrumbs.

Beat the eggs, milk and mustard together until well mixed, and stir into the flour mixture with a table knife. Lightly knead the dough on a lightly floured work surface until smooth.

Working quickly, roll out the dough to 2.5 cm thick. Cut into rounds with a 5-cm plain or fluted round pastry cutter. Bring any spare dough together, and roll out once again to cut out more scones.

Place the scones on a floured baking sheet, then brush with a little milk and sprinkle with the cheese. Bake in the centre of the oven for 10–15 minutes until risen and golden on the top and bottom.

Serve the scones straight from the oven or cool on a wire rack. Serve within 2–3 hours to enjoy them at their best. Alternatively, freeze when cool. Defrost when needed, just before eating, refresh in a hot oven for 10 minutes.

# CHOCOLATE, BEETROOT & RASPBERRY CUPCAKES DRIZZLED WITH DARK CHOCOLATE

• MAKES 12

110 g caster sugar
30 g cocoa powder, sifted
55 g rice flour
25 g cornflour
2 tsp gluten-free baking powder
3 large eggs
110 g butter or dairy-free baking margarine, softened
1 heaped tbsp blackcurrant jam
100 g beetroot, coarsely grated
75 g fresh raspberries

• FOR THE CHOCOLATE DRIZZLE

100 g good-quality dark chocolate, broken into bits
freeze-dried raspberry pieces and 3 fresh raspberries per cake, to decorate

**These delicious and nutritious little cakes are also great made with blackcurrants in place of raspberries. Decorate the cakes, simply, drizzled with chocolate, or make these cakes fit for a celebration, topped with swirls of chocolate buttercream icing with 2 teaspoons of cassis whisked in. (For buttercream icing, see page 186.)**

Preheat the oven to 200°C. Place 12 large cupcake cases in a 12-hole muffin tray.

Place the sugar, cocoa, rice flour, cornflour, baking powder, eggs and butter into a medium bowl, and beat until smooth.

Mix the jam with the beetroot, and stir into the cake batter. Fold in the fresh raspberries.

Three-quarter fill the cupcake cases with the cake batter, and bake in the oven for 15–20 minutes until the cakes are well risen and feel springy in the centre. Cool on a wire rack.

Meanwhile, melt the chocolate in a bowl set over a pan halffilled with boiling water. Using a teaspoon, drizzle the melted chocolate back and forth over the top of each cupcake.

Before the drizzled chocolate sets, sprinkle with dried raspberry pieces and arrange raspberries in the centre of each cake.

# COURGETTE, RAISIN & ALMOND CAKES TOPPED WITH ORANGE MASCARPONE ICING

• MAKES 12

50 g raisins
2 tbsp orange juice
1 tbsp honey
3 large eggs
65 g rice flour
35g cornflour
65 g ground almonds
2 tsp baking powder
80 g light brown sugar
110 g butter, softened
30 g flaked almonds, toasted and roughly chopped
125 g courgettes, grated
grated zest of 1 orange

• FOR THE MASCARPONE ICING

3 tbsp mascarpone
2 tbsp icing sugar
grated zest of 1 orange
1 tbsp freshly squeezed orange juice
2 tbsp toasted and roughly chopped flaked almonds.

**The flavours in these lovely little cakes are reminiscent of the Mediterranean. Enjoy them as they are straight from the oven, or top with orange mascarpone icing for an indulgent treat. The children will enjoy courgette, possibly for the first time, too!**

Preheat the oven to 200°C, and place 12 large cupcake cases in a 12-hole muffin tray.

Place the raisins, orange juice and honey in a pan, and bring to the boil. Simmer for 4–5 minutes until the raisins are plump and have absorbed the liquid.

Whisk the eggs, flours, ground almonds, baking powder, sugar and butter in a large bowl until smooth. Fold in the flaked almonds, courgettes, raisins and orange zest. Spoon the mixture into the paper cases until three-quarters full.

Bake the cupcakes in the oven for 15–20 minutes until they are risen and firm in the centre. Remove the cakes from the tins and cool on a wire rack.

To make the mascarpone icing, mix the mascarpone, icing sugar, orange zest and juice together until smooth. Heap onto the cooled cakes and sprinkle with the flaked almonds. Serve immediately.

# SQUIDGY CHOCOLATE & WALNUT BROWNIES

**These moist and dangerously delicious cakes taste best served warm, fresh out of the oven, with vanilla ice cream. Serve at room temperature for tea or cut into bite-sized squares for children's parties.**

- MAKES 16

85 g dark chocolate, 70% cocoa solids
110 g butter or dairy-free baking margarine
50 g potato flour
225 g granulated sugar
1 tsp gluten-free baking powder
½ tsp salt
3 medium eggs, beaten
110 g walnuts or pecans, roughly chopped

Preheat the oven to 180°C. Line a 20 cm x 20 cm square baking tin with lightly oiled greaseproof paper that stands 2–3 cm above the tin on all sides.

In a medium pan over a low heat, melt the chocolate and butter together, stirring until smooth. Remove from the heat and keep warm.

Mix the potato flour, sugar, baking powder and salt together.

Beat the eggs into the melted chocolate mixture with a wooden spoon. Quickly stir in all the dry ingredients until the batter is smooth. Stir in the chopped nuts.

Pour the batter into the prepared tin, and bake in the middle of the oven for 20–30 minutes until the centre is almost set.

Remove from the oven and leave the brownie mixture to set in the tin for 10 minutes, before cutting into squares. Either serve the brownies warm or cool on a wire rack. Store in an airtight container for up to 3 days.

*Tip*

**For variation, replace the nuts with chocolate chips or raisins.**

# MADELEINES

- MAKES 12

100 g butter or dairy-free margarine
2 tsp runny honey
zest of 1 lemon
1 tsp vanilla essence
3 medium eggs
65 g caster sugar
30 g soft brown sugar
55 g rice flour
55 g cornflour
2 tsp baking powder
icing sugar, to decorate

**These buttery little cakes are a staple teatime snack in France and Spain, and are also perfect to serve with ice cream and berries, or Spiced Blueberry Compote (page 25) and crème fraîche.**

Gently melt the butter with the honey and lemon zest, and set aside to cool. Stir in the vanilla essence.

Whisk together the eggs and sugar in a bowl until frothy. Sift the flours and baking powder over the top and whisk again until smooth. Whisk in the butter and honey mixture, and leave to stand for at least 20 minutes, but preferably for 1–2 hours.

Preheat the oven to 200°C, and brush the moulds of a large 12-hole madeleine tray with melted butter.

Pour the batter into the madeleine moulds to just below the rim.

Bake in the oven for 10–15 minutes until the madeleines are golden and risen, and feel firm and springy in the centre.

Turn out the madeleines onto a wire rack, then dust the scalloped side with icing sugar. Serve warm or within a few hours of baking.

**The batter develops a complex flavour if it is left, covered, for 1 hour at room temperature, before pouring into the moulds and baking.**

# ALMOND & HAZELNUT MACARONS FILLED WITH SALTED BUTTER CARAMEL

**Serve these delicate biscuits as they are, with ice cream and fresh fruit, or sandwiched together with salted butter caramel, lemon curd or raspberry jam for petit fours.**

- MAKES 18

30 g hazelnuts
170 g icing sugar
90 g ground almonds
3 medium egg whites
60 g caster sugar

- FOR THE SALTED BUTTER CARAMEL FILLING

60 g caster sugar
20 g salted butter, diced
100 ml double cream

Preheat the oven to 180°C, and line a baking tray with greaseproof paper. Toast the hazelnuts for 10 minutes.

Leave the nuts to cool for 5 minutes, then pour into a tea towel and rub off the skins. Finely grind the blanched nuts in a food processor (pulse several times to achieve the right texture, wiping down the bowl and blades with a spatula in between if needed, to avoid making butter).

Mix the icing sugar, ground almonds and hazelnuts together in a large bowl.

In a separate large bowl, beat the egg whites with the caster sugar until the meringue is very stiff with a pearly sheen.

Stir half of the meringue into the nut mixture. Stir in the remaining meringues to form a smooth and shiny mixture.

Pipe 36 small rounds, 2.5 cm in diameter, at regular, well-spaced intervals onto the lined baking tray. Bake in the oven for 12–15 minutes until lightly golden on top. Peel the macarons off the baking parchment and transfer to a wire rack to cool.

Meanwhile, to make the salted butter caramel, first melt the caster sugar in a medium pan over a medium heat. Continue to cook, swirling the pan periodically but not stirring, until the sugar has caramelized to a rich golden brown colour.

Gradually swirl in the diced butter and cream, then stir continuously until the mixture is smooth and shiny. Simmer gently for a further 5 minutes, then remove from the heat and pour into a bowl to cool and thicken.

To assemble the macarons, sandwich 1 teaspoon of the salted caramel between the bases of 2 macarons. Continue until all the macarons have been sandwiched together. Serve within 2 hours of filling, or store the individual biscuits for up to 24 hours, before assembling and serving.

# SPICED APPLE, SULTANA, NUT & POPPY SEED PUFF PASTRY SWIRLS

**These pretty puff pastry swirls are chewy and wholesomely good to eat for brunch. Serve them straight from the oven or store for up to 3 days in an airtight container, and refresh in a hot oven before eating.**

- MAKES 12

1 x 400-g block gluten-free puff pastry, defrosted to room temperature

- FOR THE FILLING

2 Granny Smith apples, peeled, cored and coarsely grated
25 g flaked almonds
25 g hazelnuts roughly chopped
1 tbsp poppy seeds
2 handfuls sultanas
2 tbsp runny honey
1 tsp ground cinnamon
1 tsp mixed spice

- TO DECORATE

1 tbsp honey for drizzling
1 tbsp flaked almonds
1 tbsp poppy seeds

Preheat the oven to 180°C.

Roll out the pastry into a rectangle 2–3 mm thick and approximately 25 cm x 35 cm.

Mix the filling ingredients together, and spread evenly over the pastry leaving a border of 1 cm around the edges.

Working from a longer side of the pastry rectangle, tightly roll up like a Swiss roll.

With a sharp knife, cut the roll into about 12 slices, each 2 cm thick. Place on a baking tray, and drizzle a little honey over each swirl, then sprinkle with the almonds and poppy seeds.

Bake in the oven for 20 minutes, or until the pastry has puffed and is crisp and golden brown in the centre of each swirl.

Serve straight out of the oven or cooled to room temperature.

# CRANBERRY & WHITE CHOCOLATE CHIP COOKIES

• MAKES 18

- 110 g butter or dairy-free baking margarine, softened
- 110 g granulated sugar
- 110 g soft light brown sugar
- 1 medium egg, beaten
- 85 g rice flour
- 85 g ground almonds
- 1 tsp gluten-free baking powder
- ½ tsp salt
- 1 tbsp milk or dairy-free milk
- 60 g good-quality white chocolate, roughly chopped or an alternative dairy-free ingredient
- 60 g dried cranberries, roughly chopped

**Great for teatime, packed lunches and children's parties. Try replacing the cranberries with raisins or chopped nuts, and the white chocolate with milk chocolate, or make dairy-free cookies by using dark chocolate chips. For a really indulgent treat that children love, sandwich the cookies together with vanilla or chocolate ice cream.**

Preheat the oven to 180°C.

Lightly brush 3 baking trays with vegetable oil, then shake a spoonful of rice flour around each baking tray until it is evenly covered; tip away the excess.

Beat the butter and granulated and light brown sugars with a wooden spoon or electric whisk until pale and fluffy. Add the egg and beat well.

Sift the rice flour, ground almonds, baking powder and salt into the bowl, and whisk into the creamed butter mixture. Stir in the milk. The biscuit mixture should be soft and smooth.

Stir in the chocolate and cranberries.

Spoon no more than 6 heaped teaspoons of the mixture onto each lined baking tray, leaving a wide gap between cookies – the dough spreads as it cooks.

Place the cookies on the middle shelf of the oven, and bake for 10–15 minutes until they are lightly browned and just set in the centre. Do not overcook, or the biscuits will lose their chewiness.

Once the biscuits are baked, allow them to set on the baking tray for 30 seconds, then lift onto a wire rack while they are still pliable, to cool and harden.

These cookies are best served freshly made, but can be stored for up to 2 days in an airtight container. They can also be frozen, sealed in plastic bags and defrosted when needed.

# ALMOND, PISTACHIO & LEMON BISCOTTI

**These crisp, aromatic biscuits finish a meal beautifully, dipped into a liqueur of your choice. Alternatively, serve with creamy or fruity desserts, or dip into a strong cup of coffee. Biscoti are wonderful served very fresh, and can also be stored for up to a week in an airtight container.**

- MAKES 25

75 g blanched whole almonds
75 g shelled pistachio nuts
3 large eggs
zest of 1 lemon
150 g rice flour
150 g cornflour
110 g ground almonds
150 g caster sugar
1 tsp baking powder
pinch of salt

Preheat the oven to 180°C. Spread the blanched almonds and shelled pistachios over the bottom of a roasting tray. Bake for 8–10 minutes until lightly browned and fragrant. Set aside to cool, then coarsely chop.

Reduce the oven temperature to 150°C, and line a baking sheet with greaseproof paper.

In a small bowl, lightly beat the eggs and lemon zest together. Set aside.

In a separate bowl combine the rice flour, cornflour, ground almonds, sugar, baking powder, salt and chopped almonds and pistachios.

Gradually stir the egg mixture into the dry ingredients and beat until a dough forms. Knead lightly to form a smooth dough.

On a work surface lightly dusted with cornflour, roll out the dough into a cylinder about 35 cm long and 8 cm wide. Cut the cylinder in half across its length, and place each cylinder, well apart on the prepared baking tray. The biscuit dough will spread outwards as it bakes. Bake in the middle of the oven for 30–40 minutes until firm and golden brown.

Cut the baked dough across into slices 1.5 cm thick, and arrange the slices in a single layer on the base of the baking tray. Bake the biscotti for a further 10 more minutes on each side, or until they are crisp and firm, then transfer to a wire rack to cool.

Serve immediately or store in an airtight container for up to 1 week.

*Tip*

**For variation, replace the pistachio nuts with blanched hazelnuts or chocolate chips, and the lemon zest with orange zest.**

# SAVOURY CHEESE SABLÉS WITH DIJON & ROSEMARY

- MAKES 30 SMALL OR 15 LARGE

100 g rice flour
50 g fine polenta
75 g cornflour
1 large pinch of salt
1 tbsp finely chopped fresh rosemary leaves
225 g cold butter, diced
225 g mature Cheddar cheese, finely grated
1 tsp Dijon mustard
1 medium egg, beaten, plus one extra, beaten, to glaze
1 tbsp poppy seeds
freshly ground black pepper

**These rich and cheesy melt-in-the-mouth savoury biscuits are delicious made small to serve with drinks or in larger rounds to serve with soup, cold meats and salad. Don't eat too many if you are worried about your waistline.**

Preheat the oven to 200°C.

Sift the rice flour, polenta, cornflour, salt and 3 grinds of black pepper into a large bowl, and stir in the rosemary.

Rub the butter into the dry ingredients to form a mixture that looks like coarse breadcrumbs, then stir in the cheese.

Mix the mustard and 1 beaten-egg together, then stir into the dry ingredients with a table knife. Lightly and quickly knead the biscuit dough until it comes together as a smooth ball.

Lightly dust the work surface with cornflour, and roll out the dough out to 5 mm thick. Stamp out into a rounds with a small- or medium-sized pastry cutter and arrange, well spaced apart to allow for spreading, on 2 baking trays. Brush with the egg and sprinkle with the poppy seeds.

Bake in the oven for 10–15 minutes until the biscuits are golden brown. Leave to cool for 5 minutes on the trays, then transfer to a wire rack to cool.

Serve immediately or store for up to 3 days in an airtight container. The biscuits can also be frozen. Defrost, then refresh in a hot oven for 5 minutes before serving.

# DRIED FRUIT, SEED & NUT GRANOLA BARS

- MAKES 24

100 g gluten-free rolled oats
40 g flaxseed
40 g sunflower seeds
20 g chia seeds
50 g ground almonds
50 g cornfour
50 g rice flour
200 g golden caster sugar
pinch of salt
100 g dates, roughly chopped
100 g dried apricots, roughly chopped
25 g hazelnuts, roughly chopped
25 g pistachio nuts, roughly chopped
1 tsp gluten-free baking powder
1 tsp ground cinnamon
125 g butter or dairy-free baking margarine
40 g runny honey

**These nourishing bars are the perfect solution for breakfast on the go or for an energy boost during the day. They will stay fresh for up to one week if stored in an airtight container.**

Preheat the oven to 180°C, and line a large ovenproof baking dish, 30 cm x 25 cm, with baking paper.

Mix the oats, seeds, ground almonds, flours, sugar, salt, dates, apricots and nuts in a bowl. Set aside.

In a small pan, melt the butter, honey and 1 tablespoon water together until well blended. Stir in the baking powder and ground cinnamon.

Pour the butter and honey mixture over the dry ingredients and mix well.

Spread and press the granola mixture to an even depth over the bottom of the prepared baking tray. Bake in the oven for 30 minutes, or until golden brown.

Remove from the oven and leave to cool completely, then slice into 24 bars.

Store in an airtight container for up to 1 week.

*Tip*

**For variety, try making these bars with other dried fruits such as cranberries and blueberries in place of the dates and apricots. You could experiment with the seeds and nuts too.**

# OAT, COCONUT & FRUIT FLAPJACKS

**These are healthy feel-good flapjacks where the goodness of oats is enhanced with coconut, dried fruit and, if you would like to add them, chopped nuts.**

- MAKES 20–24

100 g gluten-free rolled oats
80 g dessicated coconut
50 g buckwheat flour
100 g cornflour
200 g soft light brown sugar
1 tsp gluten-free baking powder
pinch of salt
60 g raisins
80 g chopped apricots
60 g chopped dates
30 g flaked almonds (optional)
125 g butter or dairy-free baking margarine
30 g golden syrup

Preheat the oven to 180°C, and line an ovenproof baking dish, 30 cm x 25 cm, with greaseproof paper.

In a large bowl, mix together the oats, coconut, buckwheat flour, cornflour, sugar, baking powder, salt, dried fruit and almonds (if using).

In a small pan, gently heat the butter, golden syrup and 1 tablespoon water, stirring until well blended. Pour into the dry ingredients and mix well.

Tip the flapjack mixture into the prepared baking dish and spread out evenly. Gently press over the bottom of the dish to an even thickness.

Bake in the centre of the oven for 30 minutes, or until slightly risen and golden brown. Remove from the oven and leave to cool in the dish until only slightly warm. Using a sharp knife into 20–24 squares and leave to cool completely.

Serve immediately or store in an airtight container for up to 1 week.

# SPICED CARROT, PARSNIP & ORANGE CAKE

**This cake persuades children to eat their vegetables with pleasure. For individual cakes, divide the mixture among cupcake cases. Double the recipe for a tall, café-style sandwich carrot cake.**

- SERVES 8

110 g butter or dairy-free baking margarine, softened
55 g rice flour
55 g cornflour
110 g light brown muscovado sugar
2 tsp gluten-free baking powder
pinch salt
1 tsp ground cinnamon
½ tsp freshly grated nutmeg
½ tsp mixed spice
3 medium eggs, at room temperature
zest of 1 orange
100 g carrot, grated
100 g parsnip, grated
50 g raisins
40 g pecans, roughly chopped

- FOR THE ORANGE CREAM CHEESE ICING

50 g butter, softened
250 g cream cheese
275 g icing sugar, sifted
zest of 1 orange and
1 tbsp freshly squeezed orange juice
20 g pecans, roughly chopped

Preheat the oven to 180°C. Grease a 20-cm springform cake tin with butter or dairy-free baking margarine and line with greaseproof paper.

Place the butter, flours, sugar, baking powder, salt, spices, eggs and orange zest in a medium bowl. Whisk together on a medium speed until the mixture is smooth and well blended.

With a large metal spoon, fold in the carrot, parsnip, raisins and pecans. Tip the mixture into the prepared cake tin, and bake in the oven for 30–35 minutes until the centre is set and springy, and a skewer inserted into the middle of the cake comes out clean.

Remove from the oven, then peel off the lining paper and leave to cool in the tin on a wire rack. When cold, run a sharp knife around the edge of the cake, and transfer from the tin and to a serving plate.

To make the icing, in a large bowl, whisk the butter until soft and fluffy, then whisk in the cream cheese, icing sugar and orange zest and juice, until smooth and thick. Spread over the cooled cake. Sprinkle with the chopped pecans, and serve.

*Tip*

**To make a dairy-free icing, mix 300 g softened dairy-free baking margarine, beat 275 g icing sugar, the finely grated zest of 1 orange and the finely grated zest of 1 lime together – and add 1 tablespoon of lime juice to give the icing a citrus kick.**

# CHOCOLATE SWISS ROLL FILLED WITH RASPBERRIES & CREAM

- SERVES 4–6

4 medium eggs, separated
170 g icing sugar
55 g cocoa powder

- FOR THE FILLING

175 ml whipping cream
1 tbsp icing sugar
100 g raspberries, blackberries, blackcurrants, blueberries, sliced strawberries, or stoned and halved black cherries
icing sugar, for dusting

**This is another recipe using a fat-free sponge, which makes it very light to eat. It does not keep, so don't feel guilty tucking in. Chocolate swiss roll can be eaten as it is with a cup of tea or served as a dessert with raspberry sauce (page 145) or Spiced Blueberry Compote (page 25).**

Preheat the oven to 200°C, and line a 23 cm x 30 cm Swiss roll tin with greaseproof paper standing proud of the tin by 3 cm on all sides.

In a large bowl, whisk the egg yolks with half of the icing sugar until thick and creamy.

Clean the whisks thoroughly and, in a clean, dry bowl whisk the egg whites until they form firm peaks that do not wobble when the bowl is shaken. Add half of the remaining icing sugar and continue to whisk the egg whites until they form stiff peaks. Stir 2 large spoonfuls of egg white into the whisked egg yolk mixture to loosen it, then fold in the remaining egg white.

Mix the cocoa powder and remaining icing sugar together, and sift over the whisked egg mixture. Gently fold into the foamy mixture until just blended.

Pour the chocolate sponge mixture into the prepared tin, and gently spread out over the bottom of the tin using a palette knife.

Bake in the oven for 8–10 minutes until the sponge is lightly set and feels springy in the centre. Remove from the oven and cool on a wire rack covered with a clean, dampened tea towel, to prevent it from drying out.

Meanwhile, get ready to assemble and roll the cake. To make the filling, whip the cream with the icing sugar until it just holds its shape. Place a large sheet of greaseproof paper dusted with icing sugar on the work surface. Turn the chocolate sponge out onto the sugared greaseproof paper. Peel off the lining paper used for baking the sponge.

Spread the sponge with the whipped cream, leaving a clear border 3 cm wide around the edge of the sponge. Scatter over the raspberries.

To roll the Swiss roll, place a short edge of the Swiss roll square with the work surface. Fold the shortest edge furthest from you, 3 cm over the

*Tip*

**Try replacing raspberries with other fresh summer fruits or simply with jam.**

cream. Hold on to the greaseproof paper under the folded edge, using it to support the sponge as you slowly roll the sponge towards you.

Once rolled, transfer the Swiss roll to a serving plate using the greaseproof paper as support. Dust with extra icing sugar, and serve in thick slices.

# LEMON DRIZZLE CAKE

- SERVES 6–8

190 g unsalted butter or dairy-free baking margarine, softened
190 g golden caster sugar
6 medium eggs, at room temperature
30 g polenta
110 g rice flour
75 g cornflour
3 tsp gluten-free baking powder
grated zest of 1 lemon

- FOR THE LEMON DRIZZLE GLAZE

juice of 1 lemon
100 g golden caster sugar

**This sunny yellow, lemony cake is a favourite. Make it either in a loaf tin or as a tray-bake.**

Preheat the oven to 180°C, and line a 1-litre loaf tin or ovenproof baking dish with greaseproof paper, and brush lightly with vegetable oil.

Place the butter, sugar, eggs, polenta, flours, baking powder and lemon zest in a large bowl, and whisk on a medium speed until the cake batter is smooth. Pour the batter into the prepared tin.

Bake the cake in the centre of the oven for 30–40 minutes until the cake feels springy in the centre when gently pressed and a skewer inserted into the middle of the cake comes out clean. Remove from the oven and turn out of the tin onto a wire rack, standing over a tray, to cool.

While the cake is still hot, make the lemon drizzle glaze. Briefly stir the lemon juice and sugar together and, before the sugar has fully dissolved, spoon over the cake. Leave the cake to cool completely and serve in thick slices.

# WHISKED SPONGE FILLED WITH CREAM & STRAWBERRIES

- SERVES 6–8

4 medium eggs
110 g caster sugar
110 g cornflour
pinch of salt
4 tsp warm water
1 heaped tsp gluten-free baking powder

- FOR THE FILLING

2 heaped tbsp good-quality strawberry jam
200 ml whipping cream
200 g strawberries, thinly sliced lengthways
icing sugar for dusting

- TO PREPARE THE TIN

vegetable oil for greasing
1 tbsp caster sugar
1 tbsp cornflour

**A fat-free, feather-light sponge cake and an impressive treat for tea. Fill simply with strawberry or raspberry jam, or go the whole hog with cream and strawberries.**

Preheat the oven to 190°C.

To prepare the tins to ensure this delicate sponge does not stick, lightly grease two 20-cm springform tins with vegetable oil and line the bases with lightly oiled greaseproof paper. Take one of the tins, sprinkle in the caster sugar and shake around the tin until the side and bottom are evenly covered. Tip the excess sugar out into the second oiled tin and do the same again. Sprinkle in the cornflour, and shake around the tins in the same way, to evenly cover the sugared bottoms and sides. Tip out the excess flour and discard.

To make the sponge cakes, place the eggs and sugar in a large heatproof bowl, set on the rim of a pan half-filled with simmering water. Whisk the eggs and sugar together on high speed to a thick, creamy foam that holds its shape. This could take 10–15 minutes.

Remove from the heat and whisk in the warm water.

Sift the cornflour, baking powder and salt together into a bowl. Sift half of the flour onto the whisked eggs. Using a large metal spoon, gently fold the flour into the whisked egg, then fold in the remaining flour.

Gently spoon the cake mixture into the prepared tins, and bake in the centre of the oven for 30 minutes, or until the cakes are well risen and the centre of the cakes feel firm and springy when pressed gently.

Turn the cakes out onto a wire rack to cool, and remove the lining paper.

When cool, transfer one of the cakes, risen side down, to a serving plate. Spread with the jam. Whisk the cream until it just holds its shape and spread evenly over the jam. Arrange slices of strawberries in 1 or 2 layers on the cream, then top with the second sponge cake.

(For a simpler cake, spread one sponge with jam, then top with the second sponge cake.)

Dust with icing sugar, and serve in generous slices.

# STICKY TREACLE & GINGER LOAF CAKE

- SERVES 6–8

110 g butter or dairy-free baking margarine
110 g muscovado sugar
110 g black treacle
70g rice flour
50 g cornflour
2 tsp ground ginger
1 tsp ground cinnamon
50 g ground almonds
3 medium eggs, beaten
2 lumps of stem ginger, diced finely
70 ml milk or dairy-free milk
2 tsp bicarbonate of soda

**This is a moist and richly flavoured batter cake, perfect for elevenses. It's a really good recipe to make with children because they love stirring the foaming milk into the batter. This cake improves over 5 days – if it lasts that long.**

Preheat the oven to 150°C, and place a paper loaf cake liner inside a 1 kg loaf tin.

Heat the butter, sugar and treacle together in a pan until the sugar has completely dissolved. Remove from the heat and cool to room temperature.

Meanwhile, sift the rice flour, cornflour, ground ginger and ground cinnamon into a bowl, then mix in the ground almonds.

When the sugar mixture is cool, stir in the beaten eggs, then beat in the flours and spices. Stir in the diced stem ginger.

Warm the milk to tepid in a clean pan and stir in the bicarbonate of soda. The milk will start to fizz and foam. To make the most of the bubbles stir it quickly into the cake mixture until well blended.

While the cake mixture is still foaming, pour it into the lined loaf tin and bake in the centre of the oven for 45 minutes, or until the centre of the cake feels firm and springy when pressed and a skewer inserted into the middle of the cake comes out clean.

Cool for 10 minutes in the loaf tin, then turn the cake out onto a wire rack. Once the cake is cool, serve in thick slices.

*Tip*

**For a lighter tasting version, replace half the black treacle with golden syrup.**

# WALNUT, DATE, BANANA & HONEY CAKE

**This is a really nutritious and flavoursome cake to enjoy with a cup of tea or as a welcome energy-giving snack when out and about. This cake can be stored for up to a week in an airtight container.**

- SERVES 8

50 g pitted dates, roughly chopped
1 tbsp freshly squeezed orange juice
110 g rice flour
55 g cornflour
55 g ground walnuts
4 tsp gluten-free baking powder
1 tsp ground cinnamon
220 g butter or dairy-free baking margarine, softened
100 g soft light brown sugar
2 tbsp runny honey
4 medium eggs
1 large ripe banana or 2 small bananas, mashed
zest of 1 orange
40 g walnuts roughly chopped
1 tbsp demerara sugar

Preheat the oven to 170°C, and place a paper loaf cake liner inside a 1-kg loaf tin.

Mix the dates with the orange juice, and set aside for 15 minutes.

Meanwhile, tip the flours, ground walnuts, baking powder, cinnamon, butter, sugar, honey, eggs, mashed bananas and orange zest into a large bowl. Beat together until smooth.

Stir in the soaked dates (with any juice) and chopped walnuts. Spoon the cake mixture into the lined loaf tin, level out with a spoon and sprinkle with the demerara sugar.

Bake in the oven for 1 hour, or until the centre feels firm and springy, and a skewer inserted into the middle of the cake comes out clean.

Remove from the oven and cool in the tin for 10 minutes, then turn the cake out of the tin onto a wire rack to finish cooling.

Remove the lining paper, and serve the cake cut into thick slices.

# SQUIDGY CHOCOLATE, ALMOND & PRUNE TORTE

- SERVES 8–10

55 g ready-to-eat pitted prunes, roughly chopped
50 ml brandy or Amaretto
3 medium eggs, separated
140 g caster sugar
200 g dark chocolate, 70% cocoa solids, roughly chopped
110 g unsalted butter or dairy-free baking margarine, diced
100 g ground almonds
40 g cornflour
oil, for greasing

**This rich and fruity torte was a particular favourite among the American and British art and architecture tourists I catered for in Tuscany many moons ago, and it stands the test of time with friends and family now. Serve with double cream or crème fraîche.**

Soak the prunes in the brandy for 30 minutes.

Preheat the oven to 180°C. Grease a 20-cm springform tin with butter and line the base with greased greaseproof paper.

Beat the egg yolks with the caster sugar on high speed until thick and creamy.

Place the chocolate and 2 tablespoons of water in an ovenproof bowl, sitting on the rim of a small pan of simmering water. Stir the melting chocolate and water together until smooth. Slowly incorporate the butter, a few pieces at a time, to form a smooth, shiny liquid.

Pour the melted chocolate mixture over the whisked egg yolks, and gently fold together using a large metal spoon.

Sift the ground almonds and cornflour over the chocolate mixture, add the soaked prunes and brandy, and gently fold through.

In a clean, dry bowl, whisk the egg whites until they form firm peaks that do not wobble when the bowl is shaken. Stir a large spoonful into the chocolate mixture, then gently fold in the remaining egg whites.

Pour the mixture into the prepared tin, and bake in the centre of the oven for 35–40 minutes until the centre of the torte is just set. Leave to get cool in the tin on a wire rack.

Run a sharp knife around the edge of the torte, remove the tin and lining paper, and transfer the torte to a serving dish.

Serve in narrow slices with double cream or a dollop of crème fraîche on the side. Your guests can always come back for more.

# EASY CHOCOLATE SANDWICH CAKE WITH CHOCOLATE BUTTERCREAM ICING

- SERVES 6–8

170 g cornflour
60 g cocoa powder
6 medium eggs, at room temperature
220 g caster sugar
3 tsp gluten-free baking powder
220 g butter or dairy-free baking margarine, softened
1 tbsp warm water

- FOR THE CHOCOLATE BUTTERCREAM ICING

170 g unsalted butter or dairy-free baking margarine, softened
85 g cocoa powder
170 g icing sugar
1 tbsp warm water

**This quick and easy sandwich cake recipe is perfect for birthday cakes and impromptu gatherings. The sponge is also ideal for individual cupcakes or chocolate fairy cakes, topped or filled with chocolate buttercream icing. Spoon the cake batter into paper cases and bake at 180°C for 15–20 minutes. This cake tastes equally good made with dairy-free ingredients.**

Preheat the oven to 180°C. Line two 20-cm sandwich cake tins with greaseproof paper, and lightly grease with vegetable oil.

Place all the cake ingredients in a large mixing bowl, and whisk on medium speed until the batter is smooth.

Pour the batter into the prepared cake tins, and spread out evenly with a table knife. Bake in the centre of the oven for 30 minutes, or until the centre of each cake is springy.

Run a sharp knife around the edge of the cakes, and turn them out onto a wire rack, peeling off the lining paper. Leave to cool completely.

When the cakes are almost cold, make the chocolate icing. Whisk the butter until creamy, sift in the cocoa powder and icing sugar, then add the warm water. Whisk the ingredients together until the icing is smooth and creamy in consistency.

Place one of the cakes on a serving plate, risen side down, and spread with half the icing. Place the second cake, flat side down, on top. Spread the remaining icing over the top.

Serve in generous slices, and enjoy.

# INDEX

**S**



**T**



**V**



**W**



**Y**



**Z**

I dedicate the *Genius Gluten-Free Cookbook* to each and every member of Team Genius, all of whom created the unique and impressive business Genius is today.

# ACKNOWLEDGEMENTS

First, I would like to thank Victoria Marshallsay, our enterprising publishing agent, who introduced me to publishing experts Carey Smith and Lydia Good of Ebury Press. I would also like to thank Sue Roberts, James Watts, Katherine Corbett and Rebecca Wainwright from Clarion PR, and Jo Pierce and Harriet Beesley from Pearlfisher. Many thanks also to Mari Williams and Joff Lee for their beautiful food styling and photography. It has been a privilege to work with such a talented and enthusiastic team throughout the production of this beautiful book. Roz Cuschieri, Andy Ley, Steve Clarke, Elizabeth Macgregor-Smith and Ali Atkinson also sit at the heart of turning the *Genius Gluten-Free Cookbook* from a concept into reality.

I would also like thank our Board – Sir Bill Gammell, John Dunsmore, Frédéric de Mevius, Eric Melloul, Edward Murray, Stella Morse – and my colleagues Victoire Carous, Kevin Smithson, Dave Shaw, Yann Salaun and Andy Ivel for their encouragement and understanding of what it takes to bring a book such as this to fruition.

Last but not least, I would like to thank my husband, Hew, who has offered constant support during my decade-long quest to improve the quality of gluten-free products for Genius consumers, and my sons Angus, Robin and Otto, who motivated me to work in this area in the first place.

Together we have created a special book of delicious and inspiring recipes that I hope our consumers enjoy preparing over and over again for their friends and family.

Bon appétit!

LUCINDA BRUCE-GARDYNE

1 3 5 7 9 10 8 6 4 2

First published in 2016 by Vermilion, an imprint of Ebury Publishing

Ebury Press is part of the Penguin Random House group of companies whose addresses can be found at global.penguinrandomhouse.com

Penguin Random House UK



A CIP catalogue record for this book is available from the British Library

PROJECT EDITOR Victoria Marshallsay
DESIGN Lisa Pettibone
PHOTOGRAPHS Joff Lee
Printed and bound in Italy by Rotolito Lombarda SpA

ISBN 9781785040702

Penguin Random House is committed to a sustainable future for our business, our readers and our planet. This book is made from Forest Stewardship Council ® certified paper.